From CIA to APT:
An Introduction to
Cyber Security

From CIA to APT:
An Introduction to Cyber Security

Preface

Those who surrender freedom for security will not have, nor do they deserve, either one.

Benjamin Franklin

Most introductory books on cyber security are either too technical for popular readers, or too casual for professional ones. This book, in contrast, is intended to reside somewhere in the middle. That is, while concepts are explained in a friendly manner for any educated adult, the book also necessarily includes network diagrams with the obligatory references to clouds, servers, and packets.

But don't let this scare you. Anyone with an ounce of determination can get through every page of this book, and will come out better informed, not only on cyber security, but also on computing, networking, and software. While it is true that college students will find the material particularly accessible, any adult with the desire to learn will find this book part of an exciting new journey.

A great irony is that the dizzying assortment of articles, posts, and books currently available on cyber security makes it difficult to navigate the topic. Furthermore, with so much information coming from writers with questionable backgrounds in cyber security, separating the wheat from the chaff has become an almost impossible task for most readers, experienced or otherwise.

This book is written specifically to address that problem. That is, we set out to create an accessible but technically accurate work on cyber security that would not insult the intelligence of our readers. We avoid the temptation to navigate away from the technical issues, choosing instead to steer toward the detailed concepts in the hopes that our readers will develop new understanding and insights.

The material here provides a *technical grounding* that is commensurate with what you might receive in a college course on the topic. If you are an engineer, developer, or student, then you are certainly in the right place. On the other hand, if you work in management, executive leadership, or some other non-technical role, then this is exactly the technical grounding in cyber that you've been looking for.

Anyone who has not been sleeping in a cave the past few years knows the consequences of misguided decision-making in cyber security. Business leaders colliding with this complex issue will find their intellectual property gone and their services blocked by hackers. Government and political leaders who misstep in this area will find their careers, programs, and campaigns ruined.

Consider this: Target, Home Depot, and Sony have seen massive attacks on their infrastructure, and most citizens, including our leaders, have no idea how or why this occurred. Similarly, we watched data leaks from the US Office of Personnel Management and the Democratic National Committee, and most people have only a vague sense of how such cyber attacks were accomplished.

Perhaps more disturbingly, decision-makers in our society have no idea how to reduce this risk. Because they typically have zero technical understanding, they are forced to suggest simple, trite measures they can understand like awareness, penalties, and compliance. Our approach here is to demonstrate that cyber security attacks are best avoided through improved technology and architecture.

Written from the perspective of the professional cyber security executive, long-time academic, and industry analyst (Edward Amoroso), and the graduate computer science student, software developer, and occasional hacker (Matthew Amoroso), this book provides a concise *technical introduction to cyber security* that keeps things as straightforward as possible, but without veering into silly analogies.

One brief warning to expert readers: At times, we have decided to take out our scissors and trim some of the more confusing details of a given cyber security issue. We've tried in these cases to smoothen the edges to make complex concepts more accessible, hopefully without changing the essence of the technology. This is a difficult task, we discovered, and we hope only fat was removed and never bone.

In the end, our hope is that this short book will help you become more technically equipped to navigate the mine fields of misleading and incorrect cyber security information found across the Internet and on television. It is our hope that you will be in a better position to make informed decisions about anything of consequence that might be affected by the growing potential for cyber attacks.

If you successfully complete this book, you will no longer have to shrug when asked about cyber security. Rather, you will be able to lean in and offer an informed opinion based on an introductory grounding in the fundamental aspects of cyber security technology. Our goal is to expand your understanding and make you a more informed and educated adult.

We are pleased that you'll be spending time with our material. To not lose any momentum, proceed ahead and continue your reading *right now* with the first chapter on cyber threats.

1. Cyber Threats

Bad times have a scientific value. These are occasions a good learner would not miss.

Ralph Waldo Emerson

Let's start with some basic cyber threat-related concepts and their simple definitions:

Cyber security is all about reducing the risk of attacks to computers, networks, or software. Malicious actors, also known as *cyber offense*, try to attack *assets* such as websites or company networks. Cyber security *safeguards*, known collectively as *cyber defense*, are put in place to stop these attacks. Unfortunately, the defense is often just a speedbump for the offense.

To help explain these and similar concepts, cyber security experts like to draw diagrams such as the one shown below in Figure 1-1. Such diagrams offer a common visualized reference to support discussion. The diagram below depicts the offense and defense as circles, the target asset as a box, and the attack path as an arrow. As you can see, the in-line defense is designed to prevent the attack.

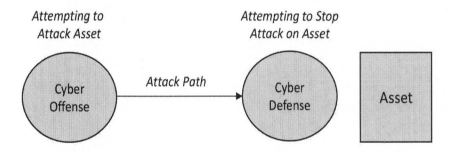

Figure 1. Cyber Offense vs. Cyber Defense

You will learn throughout this book that the cyber offense is way ahead of the cyber defense. This follows from a seemingly obvious condition: The offense must only find only *one* successful path to the target asset, whereas the defense must prevent *all* such paths. It doesn't take a technology genius to recognize that defending is therefore much harder than attacking.

This is an important issue – one that is profound, with grave implications for individuals, business, and government. Let's repeat it here for emphasis: The offense only needs to find *one way to break into your system*. The defense needs to stop *every possible break-in path*. This explains why the offense is now, and probably always will be, far ahead of the defense in cyber.

The term *threat* is used in cyber security to describe the bad things that hackers can do to assets. Three threat types exist: The first is the *confidentiality threat*, which involves sensitive information being leaked. Cyber security experts attempt to implement *privacy* controls to prevent leakage using techniques such as encryption, but this is not an easy process.

The second type is the *integrity threat*, which involves corruption of some asset. If your personal computer becomes infected with bad software called *malware*, then this is an integrity threat, albeit with limited consequences. Alternatively, if the control software in a nuclear power plant becomes infected, then the implications are more severe.

The third type of threat is known as the *availability threat*, which involves intentional blocking of access to a computer or network system. A popular blocking attack is called a *distributed denial of service* or DDOS. Websites are susceptible to DDOS attacks because they are directly connected to the Internet and can be easily reached by hackers.

Using the first three letters of these threats, cyber security experts have created the so-called *CIA model* of cyber threats, which recognizes confidentiality, integrity, and availability as the primary concerns in protecting assets. As suggested in Figure 1-2 below, virtually all cyber attacks by malicious actors will result in one or more of the threat conditions associated with the CIA model.

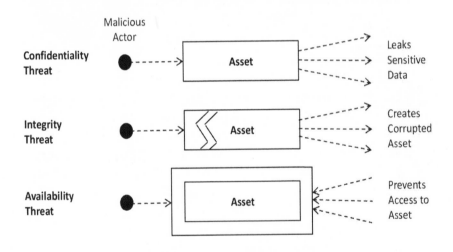

Figure 1-2. CIA Model of Cyber Threats

Some experts like to point out that *fraud* may be a fourth threat type that doesn't fit well into the CIA model. That is, if a criminal steals a service without paying, then the resulting impact doesn't fit well into disclosure, integrity, or denial of service categories. Readers should recognize that many of the "models" created in cyber security might not cover 100% of cases perfectly.

Let's now examine some familiar threat examples, starting with *confidentiality*. During the US Presidential Campaign in 2016, Democratic campaign manager, John Podesta was sloppy in his handling of email credentials. He reused passwords across multiple accounts, had unencrypted passwords sent to him across the Internet, and on and on. It was a case study in how not to manage passwords.

From this vulnerability, intruders gained access to his accounts through deceptive attacks that exposed his stored email. The result was a steady stream of leaked, embarrassing information posted to WikiLeaks that had political consequences for Podesta, Hillary Clinton, and possibly the entire United States. Most readers will have little trouble identifying other confidentiality scenarios.

An example *integrity* problem occurred at Sony Pictures several years ago. Hackers gained remote access to the Sony Pictures enterprise network through vulnerabilities in their firewall perimeter, and they used this access to attack the corporation and its employees. Specifically, they corrupted the administrative software on tens of thousands of computers, thus rendering the equipment useless.

The Sony Pictures destructive attack provides a glimpse into the frightening types of cyber issues that emerge when assets are corrupted. It also demonstrated that multiple threats can occur with one attack, because executives at Sony also had embarrassing email content exposed. The Sony incident, as is shown in Figure 1-3, was therefore a good example of a complex attack with multiple threat objectives.

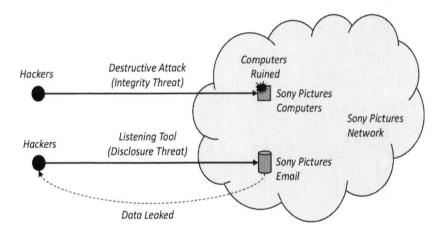

Figure 1-3. Integrity and Disclosure Threats in Sony Pictures Attack

For readers who are uncertain how to read the diagram in Figure 1-3, here are some hints: The cloud used to depict the Sony Pictures Network is just a shorthand way to designate a lot of local areas networks, computers, printers, databases, and other company resources that could not fit onto a simple diagram. You will see cloud depictions throughout this book in diagrams, and they simply hide complexity.

Furthermore, little round dots usually designate users, and boxes or cylinders usually designate resources or repositories. When we draw a line from a little dot to a little box, it means that some user or hacker "did something" to that resource. We will often label the line to explain exactly what was done. It's all very simple, and you'll get used to these diagrams as you progress with the book.

An example *availability* problem occurred in 2012 when nation-state hackers targeted banking websites with a so-called *distributed denial of service* or DDOS attack, resulting in considerable business disruption for these banks. By using a *botnet* of infected computers, the attackers overwhelmed the inbound network connections of these banks, thus preventing authorized access from customers.

Surprisingly, the DDOS attack did not go further, perhaps targeting the integrity of account information or disclosing account information to sites such as WikiLeaks. There is no good explanation for why these complementary attacks did not occur. Observers should recognize that we are experiencing the infancy of cyber threats, and that future campaigns might be considerably more troublesome.

To summarize: Cyber security is designed to prevent confidentiality, integrity, or availability threats from happening to assets like websites, networks, and applications. Since it is easier to attack something than to defend it, cyber security requires more than simple common sense solutions, as we will explain in subsequent chapters.

Our next chapter digs more deeply into the offensive techniques used to attack computer and network systems. It provides a brief introduction to the specifics around how malicious actors create *cyber attacks*.

2. Cyber Attacks

The next generation of terrorists will grow up in a digital world, with ever more powerful and easy-to-use hacking tools at their disposal.

Dorothy Denning

The process called *hacking* involves intentionally exploiting vulnerabilities. The goal is always to create a threat to a target asset. Hacking is the electronic equivalent of spotting an open window and then jumping through. The vulnerabilities exploited in a hack can range from software bugs to poorly trained staff. The steps in a hack are referred to collectively as a *cyber attack*.

Cyber attacks generally follow one of two basic patterns. They can either employ a mechanical, automated method of finding a target and then relentlessly trying everything imaginable to break in. This so-called *brute force attack* method is exemplified by software that might try to guess passwords by simply trying every conceivable guess.

The second method, called a *heuristic attack*, is considered much more powerful. It relies on human cleverness, insight, and knowledge to find clever shortcut means for gaining access. The value of a heuristic attack is often measured based on the amount of time saved for the hacker by not having to rely on the more tedious brute force method.

As one might expect, more involved cyber attacks can also be created that combine brute force and heuristic methods. Generally, when these techniques are combined into a series of steps, we refer to the result as a *hacking campaign*. When nation states perform these attacks over a long period of time, we call this an *advanced persistent attack*, or alternatively, an *advanced persistent threat* or *APT*.

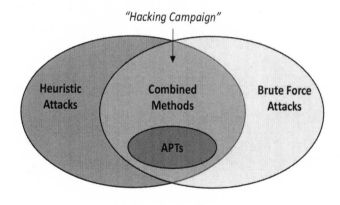

Figure 2-1. Cyber Attack Techniques

A couple of tangible examples will help to illustrate. Suppose that you are trying to crack an encryption code created to hide data from unauthorized viewers. Suppose further that you only have access to the encrypted data over a network, and that you have no other hints. It's your challenge to break the code to understand the information being sent.

If the cryptography used is like the cryptograms you might play in the newspaper, where one letter is replaced with another, then a brute force attack might be possible. If, for example, the encryption employs a Caesar-type replacement, where letters are shifted forward, say, two places forward in the English alphabet, then some example encryptions are as follows:

```
encrypt(a)=c; encrypt(b)=d; encrypt(c)=e; and so on.
```

Using this scheme, two communicating entities can encrypt plaintext messages in a manner that only exposes the so-called *ciphertext*, which involves here the English letters shifted forward two places. An example is shown below:

```
Plaintext:     the cow jumped over the moon
Ciphertext:    vjg eqy lworgf qxgt vjg oqqp
```

Unauthorized observers might try to fiddle with the ciphertext to decrypt the message, perhaps looking for patterns as one might with a cryptogram. Alternatively, this encryption scheme is vulnerable to a brute force attack, one that does not require any heuristic insights, and that can be implemented with a simple computer program.

The attack involves graphing the frequency distribution (i.e. number of occurrences) of each letter in the ciphertext. If enough ciphertext is collected and graphed, then the resultant distribution should eventually perfectly match the *real* frequency distribution of the real alphabet (see below), thus exposing the encryption replacement approach.

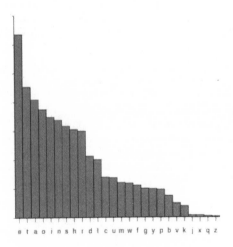

Figure 2-2. Frequency Distribution of the English Alphabet

For example, the most commonly used letters in the English alphabet are e, t, a, o, and i – in that order. If these letters are replaced in the ciphertext with g, v, c, q, and k, respectively, then their occurrence will eventually create the shapes associated with the plaintext characters they replace. Like magic, the encryption algorithm will be broken by a brute force program collecting and processing data.

Obviously, a real encryption algorithm will be orders of magnitude more complex than a simple Caesar shift cipher. Readers should recognize, however, that the brute force technique used in this example is representative of the type of processing done in even the most advanced cryptanalysis. Experts refer to this as code breaking.

A second example cyber attack involves a website that accepts user-supplied input information. For example, the site might request name, address, phone, and email information from a user, just as we have all seen thousands of times on the Internet for virtually anything you can imagine. Users type this information into the little boxes provided on the website.

The presumption in such a web form is that the programmer was careful to allow for unusual entries, such as extremely long last names or addresses. The presumption is also that the programmer accounted for cases such as snarky users holding down a key to fill up the form with repeat characters. One can easily imagine a poorly coded form exhibiting unexpected behavior in this case.

A sinister cyber attack involves the attacker knowing that web forms interact with back-end programs that accept certain types of commands. Databases, for example, generally accept standard commands called *queries*. Attackers can thus enter standard query commands into web forms in the hopes that these commands will be inadvertently passed along to the database system.

Here are the greatly simplified steps – and we mean *greatly simplified* – of how such an attack might occur: In Step 1, the hacker might enter a database query – perhaps something like "SEND ALL RECORDS" – into the form field; in Step 2, the web server might then send this unsanitized command to the database for execution; and in Step 3, if all goes as planned, the database server would respond by "sending all records" to the hacker.

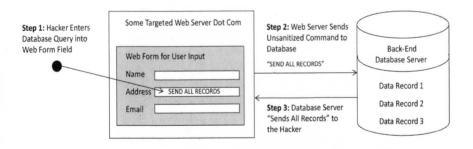

Figure 2-3. Accessing Back-End Databases via Form Commands

The result of this attack, sometimes called *SQL injection*, is that hackers can use their knowledge of weaknesses in web services to gain direct access to back-end databases containing sensitive information. This is a frightening prospect for companies who don't realize their information to anyone with an Internet connection and a browser.

Readers must know that there are literally millions of different cyber attack methods that have become well known to hackers. We include the examples above simply to illustrate brute force and heuristic approaches, but the typical cyber security practitioner will encounter more cyber attack methods in a week than could be catalogued in a thousand-page book.

What this means is that no cyber security expert can ever purport to understand all attack methods, just as no doctor can ever claim to understand all forms of disease. Like in medicine, however, good decisions on the part of the cyber defense can stop attacks that might not only be unknown, but that might not have even been invented yet.

To summarize: Hacking techniques are either brute force or heuristic. Millions of examples can be used to illustrate the concepts, but the automated breaking of a simple cipher demonstrates brute force, and the injection of database commands into a back-end server illustrates heuristic. Regardless of the strategy, hackers with browsers and Internet connections can cause considerable consequences.

In the next chapter, we introduce the types of individuals and groups that perform cyber attacks. We will see that they are driven by different motivations and purposes. Some motivations are more playful and innocent, whereas others introduce frightening and even sinister consequences, especially if an essential service is being targeted.

3. Malicious Actors

Most hackers are young because young people tend to be adaptable. As long as you remain adaptable, you can always be a good hacker.

Emmanuel Goldstein

A common question one asks with respect to cyber security is *who* specifically is doing the hacking, and *what* is their motivation. This is a reasonable attribution concern for observers, particularly ones who are familiar with the usual non-cyber law enforcement process, where crimes are investigated to identify perpetrators and bring them to justice.

Unfortunately, it is difficult to weave a traceable pattern from the victim on the Internet to the originating hacker, because the underlying protocol of the Internet – called the *Internet Protocol* or *IP*, allows sources to intentionally lie about the address from which their activity originates. That is, Alice can attack Bob using Eve's Internet persona, albeit with some limitations.

Perhaps more troublesome is that some hacker Alice can break into the system of victim 1, from which another hack can be launched to victim 2, from which another hack can be launched to victim 3, and so on – until the targeted victim is reached. The only way to trace such multi-hop hacking would be to obtain proper legal permission to investigate each intermediate hacked system.

Four Intermediate Hacked Systems on the Internet

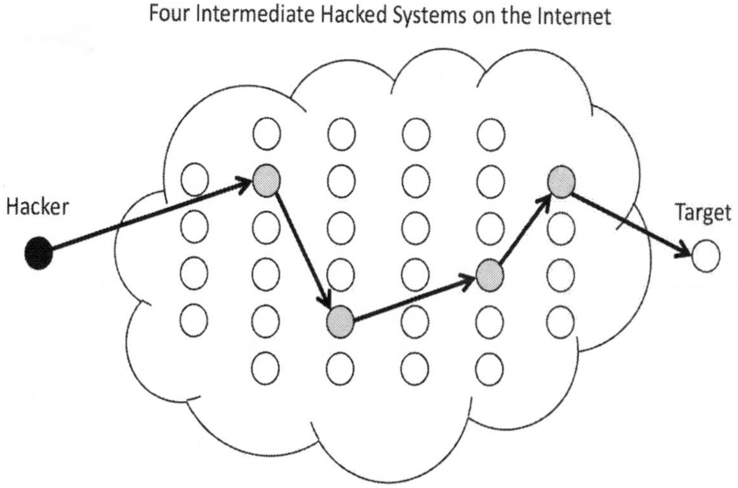

Figure 3-1. Attribution Challenge for Multi-Path Hacking

It might be tempting to expect that attribution could start with the victim and trace backward, but the intermediate systems are often inconveniently located and owned. For example, the tracing from victim to hacker could include servers in China, private systems in a corporation, or personal computers of unwitting owners. Obtaining the rights to investigate these systems is generally not possible.

Despite these challenges, decades of practical experience and empirical observation allow cyber security experts to categorize the types of malicious hackers into four groups. These groups are distinct because of differing motivation, range of offensive capability, and the degree to which they are willing to produce consequential impact to assets.

The first group includes the men and women, often still in their youth, that we would refer to as *hackers*. This might be the most interesting of all the offense groups, because participants come in three flavors: There are *white hats,* who hack to help owners, *black hats* who hack to embarrass owners, and *grey hats* who are somewhere in between. Law enforcement would be wise, by the way, to work with hackers rather than fight them.

The second group of attackers is comprised of *cyber criminals* who are motivated by money. Criminals often rely on fraudulent use of stolen accounts, and are frequently found targeting anything with financial value. This includes credit cards, medical records, and other personal information that can be sold on a hidden portion of the Internet known as the *Dark Web*.

It's worth digressing for a moment to comment on the Dark Web: Created with its own private browser known as *Tor*, the Dark Web's original motivation was to support anonymous communications. It has evolved, however, to support a somewhat hidden marketplace where questionable goods and services are marketed and sold, often with electronic money known as *Bitcoin*.

For example, if criminals steal some asset from Company XYZ, perhaps a list of customer credit cards, then they might post this stolen information to the Dark Web for sale. Nefarious buyers would then enter the Dark Web anonymously using the Tor browser to purchase the stolen goods. It's a clever marketplace that evades law enforcement in far too many cases.

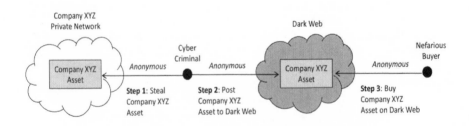

Figure 3-2. Theft and Resale of Stolen Goods on the Dark Web

Cyber security defenders dread the Dark Web, because if their private information pops up in that marketplace, then it is obvious to the world that they've been hacked. Some security vendors troll the Dark Web in search of stolen items as a service to their customers. If you download Tor and visit the Dark Web, don't be surprised if you are shocked.

The third type of attacker includes often-irresponsible actors referred to as *cyber terrorists*. Members of this group are driven by some political or philosophical motivation, and they use questionable tactics to achieve their attack go٨. ... ٧e DDOS floods aimed at the website of some in-the-crosshair organization are c٠ ٠ ٠ ٠ics of the cyber terrorist.

It is worth mentioning that cyber terrorists range in intensity from mildly motivated individuals fighting for their perception of justice, to the intensely motivated groups who are focused on real destruction. A specific group called *Anonymous* operates by suggestion and incitement, selecting targets that might include hate groups, political parties, individuals, religious organizations, and governments.

The fourth group is the *nation state attacker*, generally funded by a military organization. Nation state attackers are highly capable, supremely disciplined, and often willing to go to great lengths to use collected intelligence to damage targets. In the past, military actors would focus solely on military targets, but nation state attackers have been willing to target commercial groups.

Two specific techniques characterize typical nation state attacks: First, they involve *advanced persistent threats* (APTs) on industrial targets to steal intellectual property. The United States has seen many such attacks in recent years. Second, they involve advanced cyber weapons to disrupt, break, or deny access to an adversary's critical infrastructure. Both techniques are frightening, and the tools used are beginning to leak onto the Internet.

Returning to the earlier point that attribution is tough, most of the work that goes into determining the source of a *major* cyber attack is done by law enforcement using wiretaps, snitches, and other means to determine the source of an attack. Cyber defenders are advised generally to assume the worst, which frees them to focus their efforts on prevention rather than pure response to attacks.

To summarize: Four different groups perform hacking, ranging from hackers to nation state actors. The motivation of these groups will vary, but the reality is that responsible owners of computers, networks, and software must protect themselves from each of these groups. In that sense, it doesn't matter whether you are being targeted by teenagers or the Chinese Government. You must have defenses in place.

In the next chapter, we introduce the people and groups who are charged with the difficult task of protecting cyber assets from attack. Our presumption is that the *cyber defenders* are the good guys – the ones with grave responsibility to make sure that whatever assets they are tasked to protect are not negatively impacted by malicious actors

4. Cyber Defenders

If you spend more on coffee than IT security, then you will be hacked. What's more, you deserve to be hacked.

Richard Clarke

Just as it is reasonable to learn who is doing the hacking, it is also reasonable to learn who is doing the *defending*. Furthermore, just as any sports team would be wise to value offense and defense equally, the cyber security ecosystem would benefit from greater balance between hackers and defenders. As we've suggested earlier, however, the offense has a lopsided advantage.

In addition to the observation that attackers need only one path while defenders must prevent all paths, geographic scaling also helps the offense. That is, attacks can originate from anywhere in the world (see diagram below), but defenses must be coordinated by the local asset owner. International government and law enforcement groups might try to help, but most lack broad enough vantage points for useful assistance.

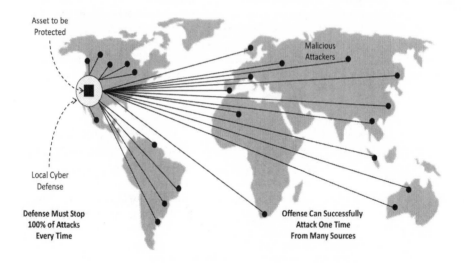

Figure 4-1. Imbalance between Cyber Offense and Defense

The types of individuals and groups involved in cyber defense can be categorized into five groups with widely varying roles, motivations, and responsibilities. These groups each play an important role in reducing the risk of cyber attacks to valued assets, albeit with different levels of authority, ownership, skill and legal protections.

The first group of defenders is the population of *individuals* on the Internet today. Each one of us has the responsibility to take reasonable precautions against cyber attacks. Like citizens who agree to prevent infectious disease through cleanliness, individuals must agree to do the same for cyber security, albeit with the provision that it's not always obvious how this is done.

Most individuals are particularly susceptible to an attack known as *phishing*. This involves sending someone an enticing web link in the hopes that they will click and download. When they do, malware infects their computer and they become an unknowing victim of remote control. A group of similarly infected computers (*bots*) tied to a common command and control (C&C) source is called a *botnet*.

The organization of a botnet involves bots that are usually scattered around the world. A normal PC or server becomes a bot when the botnet operator (a human being) manages to get remote access software installed. This allows the operator to use your mother's PC, or your file server at work, or whatever has been infected, to participate in a coordinated attack.

Some of the hacked PCs and servers are used to issue the remote commands. These systems play the role of command and control (C&C), because they command the bots in a zombie-like manner, to attack a target victim. At some designated time, the actual attack traffic is sent to the victim, who will see the incoming attack as originating from the hacked PCs, which are likely all over the world.

Readers should note that this helps explain why it is absolute nonsense when someone on CNN gravely points out on television that some cyber attack seems to have emanated from "servers in China" or from "systems of Russian origin." Certainly, the intelligence community has its methods for determining attribution, but it's not by looking at the IP address origin of an incoming botnet attack.

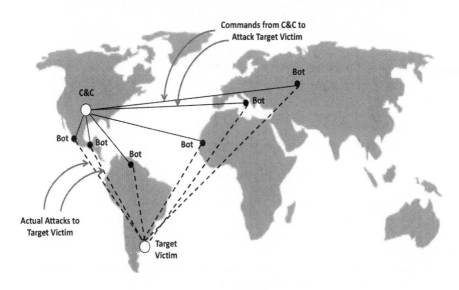

Figure 4-2. Organization of a Botnet

The second group with defensive responsibility includes the *enterprise security teams* working in companies of all sizes around the globe. Generally led by a so-called *chief information security officer (CISO)*, these groups are charged with protecting companies from cyber attacks. This includes protecting organizational PCs, applications, servers, networks, and on and on. It's a difficult job.

In most companies, the enterprise security team reports up through the chief information officer (CIO). As cyber security risk increases, however, a new trend involves making the security team more independent, and even reporting their CISO directly to the highest levels of the corporation. This trend is reminiscent of the evolution of personnel departments to more senior human resources organizations.

The third group of defenders includes the *cyber security technology vendors* who produce products and services that stop cyber attacks. Serving essentially as defensive arms dealers, this industry has grown considerably in the past few years, and many small, medium, and large vendors exist around the world to help reduce risk. Interestingly, a few vendors are now providing offensive weapons as well.

The traditional hot spot location for cyber security vendor headquarters has been Silicon Valley in California, but more recently, the industry has seen more great companies emerge from unexpected places such as Tel-Aviv and Brooklyn. We should expect to see continued growth in this industry with participants emerging from many different locations around the globe, including China and India.

The fourth group of cyber defenders includes the *government and regulatory organizations* that are trying to reduce risk through legal, policy, and oversight methods. In some cases, especially with law enforcement, there is some active involvement in dealing with cyber attacks, but most of this group's work focuses on penalties and incentives to shape behavior.

One of the more influential Federal government organizations in the US is the National Institute of Standards and Technology or NIST. The group published a popular framework recently on enterprise cyber security that helps managers and practitioners make better decisions about how they organize, manage, and respond to cyber security protection of business assets.

The resultant NIST Cybersecurity Framework provides a *core* structure for recommended activities that are organized into categories and subcategories in five protection functions. So-called tiers are included in the framework to define how much rigor an organization has with respect to the various controls (see below). One might think of the framework as a useful roadmap with checklists for improving security.

identify	Protect	Detect	Respond	Recover
Asset Management	Access Control	Anomalies and Events	Response Planning	Recover Planning
Business Environment	Awareness and Training	Continuous Monitoring	Communications	Improvements
Governance	Data Security	Detection Process	Analysis	Communications
Risk Assessment	Info Protect/Procedures		Mitigation	
Risk Management	Maintenance		Improvements	
	Protective Technology			

Figure 4-3. NIST Cybersecurity Framework

The fifth group with defensive responsibility includes *cyber military and intelligence organizations* using cyber attacks as a tactical weapon as part of their overall warfighting arsenal. As one might guess, this creates a sizable imbalance when a military command is targeting a weakly protected business. Generally, such engagements are, for the military attacker, like taking candy from a baby.

The idea that cyber security includes such military orientation is troubling, since it implies a future that will include considerable global cyber warfare activity. An obvious policy consideration for countries in the coming years will be to create and follow norms to ensure that a cyber war does not cascade out of control, possibly destroying critical infrastructure and essential services that provide safety and life-critical support.

To summarize: Five different groups are tasked with defending assets and infrastructure from cyber attacks. They range from business people protecting corporate assets to government employees dealing with attacks on national assets. These groups have varying motivations and goals, but all share one common attribute: Their jobs are challenging.

The next chapter examines the primary means by which cyber attacks are carried out – namely, *malware*. Combining the words *malicious* and *software*, malware exists because certain individual and groups are using their software skills for bad purposes. This is unfortunate, and reminds us that proper ethical standards have not been properly developed for all software and system engineers.

5. Malware

I think computer viruses should count as life. I think it says something about human nature that the only form of life we have created so far is purely destructive.

Stephen Hawking

The most fundamental tool used in cyber attacks is a type of software called *malware*. In the early days, we called this software a *computer virus*, but as the design evolved to include more advanced attack capabilities, the nomenclature evolved as well. Malware is written by malicious individuals who seek to intentionally cause bad things to happen to target assets.

Two properties enable malware: First, our computers are designed to download and execute software that was written by others. While such download is fine when the software was created by *good* developers like Microsoft or Apple, it is not fine when that software was written by *bad* developers like criminal groups. In these cases, the result is that you unknowingly install malware onto your system.

Second, you should recognize that software downloaded onto a computer is usually *trusted* to access local resources. Downloaded software can often open files, delete files, or create new files that will include code to enable attackers to connect to your system remotely. This is like allowing a stranger to enter your home, shuffle around in your things, and then invite their friends to join in.

An important difference between trusted software from good developers and malware from bad developers is whether *permission* is asked of the user. That is, when you download an app from a trusted development source, it will ask for permission to resources such as your calendar, contacts, or email. Malware, in contrast, will just go ahead and grab what it wants without the user's knowledge (see below).

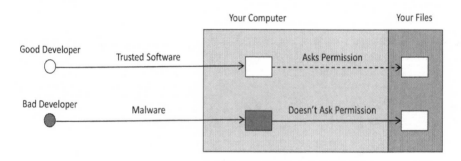

Figure 5-1. Permissions in Trusted Software vs. Malware

Any software that purports to do something good, but that also does something bad is called a *Trojan horse*. The great computer scientist, Ken Thompson, explained three decades ago while at Bell Labs that the only way to avoid Trojan horses is to avoid using software that you did not personally write. Since such a policy is impractical, Thompson correctly concluded that malware would become a serious problem.

Trojan horse design is easy to illustrate. For example, a software developer can embed hidden functions, called trap doors, into developed code. These trap doors are then invoked by anyone who knows the "secret." This simple idea is one of the fundamental notions that enables malware, because users have no choice but to trust the software they download and run.

Suppose, for example, that you are running a piece of software that includes the three simple lines of code. (By the way, if you've never read a line of software code, then relax: It is easy to follow. Each statement should be interpreted as an instruction to the computer to perform a given task. You should have little trouble understanding the general idea involved in each statement.)

```
print "type password:"
accept (password)
if valid (password) then allow
```

The purpose of this code should be obvious. That is, the software first prints onto the screen a prompt asking for the user to type a password. The software then accepts the typed password and checks to see if it is valid. If the password is valid, then the user will be allowed entry. Just about every application or system we all use includes something like this in the code.

What every hacker knows is that a Trojan horse program can be created by quietly and easily inserting a trap door with a hidden secret entry as follows:

```
print "type password:"
accept (password)
if valid (password) or password = "ABC" then allow
```

You can see from the code that if a user knows the secret password ABC, then entry will be permitted. That is, users can gain entry by having a valid password, or by knowing that the secret trap door password is ABC.

This type of secret entry is profound, because as users, we are all forced to trust the developers of our software. If developers compromise that trust, there isn't much we can do. It would be extremely rare, for example, for anyone other than a large powerful customer to be allowed to carefully review the code from a software company.

This issue of reviewing code is worth taking a moment to ponder. When you purchase a car, you have every right to lift the hood to examine the engine and other systems. Similarly, when you buy food, it is reasonable to request a label listing the ingredients. When you buy software, however, you will not have much opportunity to investigate the code that defines its operation.

There is an exception in the industry, however, known as *open source* software. This involves developers allowing the code they write to be available for open review and sharing. What's more, they agree to allow free use of the software, with the only provision that improvements be shared openly with everyone else. Traditional business people often have trouble grasping this egalitarian concept.

Let's return to the trap door example. Suppose that you download a mobile app that provides location driven services such as maps. To provide a better mapping service, the software in that app will include lines of code that look like the following:

```
ask_permission (location)
use (location) in map
```

This is exactly the sort of thing you would expect from good mapping software on your phone. It requests permission to use location services, presumably from your GPS, and then includes these location services in providing map directions. But if the mapping program included Trojan horse software, it might do the following:

```
ask_permission (location)
send (location) to developer
use (location) in map
```

When apps include this type of invasive collection of information about the user, we refer to them as *spyware*. It's almost impossible to have spent any time on the Internet without having been exposed to this sort of privacy violation. Virtually all types of malware work this way: bad code is included with good code, and the result is something quietly executing in the background without your knowledge.

One particularly interesting type of malware is known as a *worm*. Armed with the ability to self-propagate from one system to another, worm programs have been known to bring down entire networks as they gather energy jumping from one system to another, often gaining speed as they infect systems willing to accept the worm code from the Internet.

The code for a worm is surprisingly simple. It includes three lines, which are designed to find a system, send the worm, and then remotely execute the worm program on that remote system. Here is a sketch of the code, which we will call, appropriately enough, worm:

```
worm:
    find (computer)
    send (worm) to computer
    run (worm) on computer
```

Examining how this worm program runs is an example of something computer scientists call an *execution trace*. That is, we step line by line through the code and review its effects on the hosting system and network. Let's do a simple trace below, with a visualization of the effects. We assume for starters that the worm program is running on some computer called Alice.

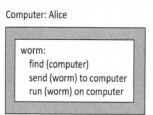

Computer: Alice

```
worm:
    find (computer)
    send (worm) to computer
    run (worm) on computer
```

When the first line of code runs on the worm program, we can see that the program has found some new computer called Bob, presumably visible over the Internet. This is easily done by testing some Internet address with a little knock on the door to see if anything answers.

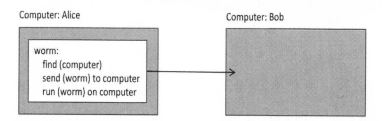

When the second line of code runs on the worm program, we can see that the actual worm_program itself has been downloaded to Bob. This is easily done using any number of software download methods, often using a browser for assistance.

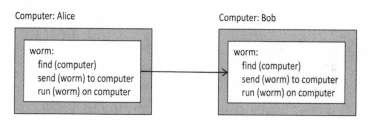

When the third line of code runs on the worm program, something interesting happens: Bob now finds a new system called Fred – and the process begins to repeat indefinitely. This step demonstrates the self-propagation aspect of a worm.

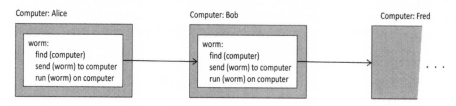

You should see from our examples that malware can range from simple spyware Trojan horses to more complex network-based programs that could have serious impact on the operations of infrastructure. Regardless of the intensity, malware preys on the trust of computer users, and should be viewed by all citizens and businesses as the product of unacceptable behavior.

To summarize: Malware is written by bad developers to cause bad things to happen to assets. Trojan horses are programs that look good, but quietly include bad functions that might involve trap door secrets. Worm programs are more involved examples of malware that can wreak more consequential havoc on bigger networks.

The coordinated set of functional, procedural, and policy-based solutions to these types of malware problems is what cyber security is all about. One of the most powerful protection concepts involves something called a *safeguard*. In the next chapter, we introduce this basic notion, which is central to all aspects of cyber security defense from attack.

Spotlight: Dorothy Denning

"I don't have a particular recommendation other than that we base decisions on as much hard data as possible. We need to carefully look at all the options and all their ramifications in making our decisions."

Dorothy Denning

Let's pause briefly from our cyber security discussion to introduce one of the great pioneers in cyber security. We will do this throughout the book, offering a Spotlight Series of little micro-biographies so that readers can develop name recognition of several pioneers who helped shaped the discipline of cyber security. We begin with a scientist who has had arguably more influence on security than any other – *Dorothy Denning*.

Born in 1945, Dorothy Denning first became interested in computers while an undergraduate at the University of Michigan in the early 1960's. Several years later, she moved along to Purdue University, where she earned the PhD degree in computer science, not to mention where she also met her future husband, Peter Denning, also a noted computer scientist.

During the early portion of her career, as the great scientists from Stanford and MIT were reporting advances in public key cryptography, Dorothy incorporated much of this work into an early computer security course she was teaching at Purdue. This culminated in 1982 in the first-ever computer security text called *Cryptography and Data Security*. Her book helped to create the field we now refer to as cyber security.

With a career that included lengthy stops at NASA Ames, SRI International, Georgetown University, and now the Naval Postgraduate School, Dorothy has made contributions to the field of cyber security that many consider unequaled. She has written more than 120 major articles and four books on the topic, and her deep involvement in shaping the US government's policies on encryption was fascinating to watch.

Anyone involved in the cyber security community owes a major debt of gratitude to Dr. Dorothy Denning for her seminal work. She continues to be a great source of inspiration, not only for all working professionals, but also for young men and women around the world who aspire to make careers in the field of protecting systems and infrastructure from cyber attacks.

6. Safeguards

When people flirt with despair, they are less likely to take the actions necessary to safeguard it, focusing instead on the short-term.

Al Gore

Returning to our cyber discussion, we now introduce the concept of *safeguards*. The goal of safeguards is to prevent cyber attacks, but the reality is that they can only reduce their risk. No reasonable person should thus expect the risk of any type of cyber attack to be zero. This is sufficiently profound to warrant a repeat: Safeguards *reduce*, but do not *remove*, the risk of cyber attacks.

Before we examine the types of safeguards available for cyber defenders, we should provide a brief illustration of how cyber security experts measure *risk*. In normal conversation, we reference risk casually, often in the context of whether it would be wise to undertake some action in our lives. We might tell a teenager that it is too risky to take the car out in the snow, for example.

In cyber security, risk is defined more carefully in terms of the following two components: First, risk involves the *probability* that a given cyber attack might occur. If, for example, an obvious defense is missing, such as a firewall not being present for a corporate network, then we would say that risk is increased due to increased probability of attack.

Second, risk involves the *consequences* that a given cyber attack might have on an asset. If, for example, a corporate network suddenly introduces a collection of important new information onto its servers, then the associated risk of attack has increased. It would be like storing expensive jewels in your basement, which obviously increases the risk of a home break-in.

Reducing the consequences of a cyber attack is not a simple task. The best approach is to remove assets, perhaps by purging extraneous copies of information that might not be needed. Another approach is to break-up and distribute a target enterprise network into smaller segments that are harder to attack. Most risk management, however, is based on the use of safeguards.

Security experts represent the relationship between risk, probability of attack, and consequences on assets by a shorthand equation:

$$\texttt{Risk = Probability X Consequence}$$
$$\texttt{(R = P X C)}$$

This shorthand equation describes the risk impact of changes in probability or consequence. For example, if P is held constant, but C is increased, then R will increase. Alternatively, if C is held constant, but P is increased, then R will also increase. If you wonder what happens if P and C move in different directions, then you begin to understand the challenges of cyber risk management.

As we've suggested, safeguards are intended to reduce cyber risk. While there are several types of safeguards, as we will explain below, they follow one of two strategies. First, safeguards can be *proactive*. This has the advantage, if it works, of preventing negative impacts from occurring. It has the disadvantage, however, of introducing something called a *false positive*.

To understand false positives, one must first understand the concept of an *indicator*. That is, when a cyber attack might be undertaken, the offense might leave some evidence of what is going on. When the defense sees this evidence, it constitutes a potential indicator or early warning of an attack. Proactive safeguards tend to make a big fuss about indicators to be more preventive.

The problem is that by making such a big fuss about every little indicator, the likelihood increases dramatically that a high percentage of these indicators turn out to be nothing at all. The situation is not unlike personal health, where you can make the decision to deal with every possible symptom, but must then accept the likelihood that many of these symptoms will be nothing at all.

Second, safeguards can be *reactive*. In such case, the safeguards are invoked only after high confidence exists that an attack has occurred, perhaps resulting in damage to a target asset. The likelihood of false positives is greatly reduced for reactive safeguards, but the possibility emerges that the consequences of waiting for an attack to unfold might be too high.

The diagram below depicts an attack moving in time from left to right, during which time, a series of indicators (indicator 1 through indicator n) are exposed to defenders. Preventive action can be taken based on the early indicators shown on the left, or responsive action can be taken based on later indicators on the right. The corresponding false positive rate is shown to drop as time progresses with the attack.

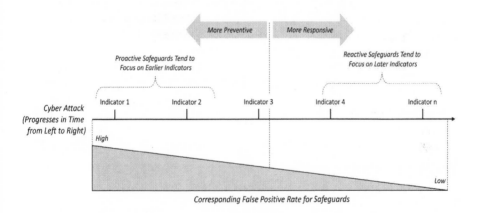

Figure 6-1. Proactive vs. Reactive Safeguards

Cyber defense consists of selecting suitable safeguards and arranging them into a comprehensive strategy for reducing risk. Safeguards come in three different categories: First, they can be *functional*, which implies real hardware and software controls that effect computing, network, or application behavior. Firewalls, encryption, and passwords are example functional safeguards.

Second, they can be *procedural*, which implies some set of agreed-upon best practices to reduce risk. The most common procedural safeguard involves methods for performing *system administration* of computer systems. This includes the decision-making around which types of services are allowed or disallowed on a given system. As you might guess, this has significant risk implications.

Finally, safeguards can involve *policy*. This is a broader category, but it includes the fines and penalties that are levied on organizations who do not demonstrate *compliance* with a set of policy rules. Policy safeguards are favored in government, because they can be applied broadly across a wide swath of different networks and systems.

The most successful defenders will tend to build their cyber defense using policy requirements as a base. They will then create their procedural and functional safeguards as a combined set of control solutions that work together to optimize risk reductions. The resulting combined layered solution is called a *cyber security architecture*.

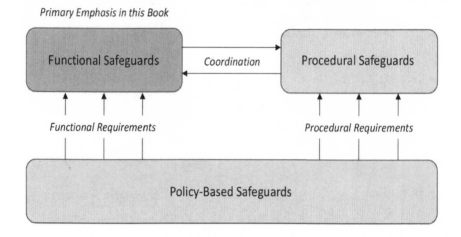

Figure 6-2. Layered Cyber Security Architecture

The specific functional controls in a cyber security architecture will tend to dominate the discussions throughout the remainder of this book. This is not intended to diminish the importance of employees being careful about how they click on various links, or how administrators should be careful about how they set up systems.

Rather, this focus on functional safeguards follows the desirable goal of using technology to prevent bad decisions from ever being made. That is, a major goal of modern cyber security is to make systems failsafe from users making a decision that might compromise assets. At the risk of sounding a bit harsh, the goal is to make systems idiot-proof. This is done with technology and architecture.

To summarize: Safeguards can be proactive or reactive, a decision that has implications on false positive rates in cyber defense. Safeguards are functional, procedural, or policy-based, but the primary emphasis in this book will be on functional controls. This follows the desirable goal to make it impossible – or at least harder – for users to make bad decisions.

The next chapter provides a foundational model called *defense in depth* that helps defenders determine how functional safeguards should be organized and combined with procedural controls to reduce cyber risk in the most efficient manner possible. No organization should even consider connecting their resources to the Internet without first understanding this layered protection approach.

7. Defense in Depth

As security or firewall administrators, we've got basically the same concerns as plumbers.

Marcus Ranum

The best cyber security architectures are based on a design approach called *defense in depth*. The idea is that if having one protective layer is good, then having two layers is better, having three is even better – and so on. While this approach might seem logically redundant, not to mention perhaps a bit expensive, years of practical experience suggest that a depth solution is imperative.

The initial instinct a security engineer might have for defense in depth would be to just double up on an existing protection, like requiring two passwords instead of one. Experts agree, however, that a more powerful means for cyber defense in depth relies on *complementary* protections, which are different, but which offer coordinated security protection.

Thus, instead of increasing depth by relying on two passwords instead of one, a better approach would be to complement the password scheme with an alternate security solution such as a firewall. The theory is that if the password scheme doesn't keep the bad guys away, then the firewall might have more luck. Effective cyber security defensive schemes are built on this fundamental notion of diverse layers.

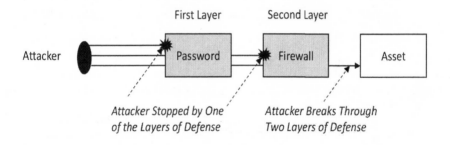

Figure 7-1. Illustration of Defense in Depth

The strength of the complementary approach to defense in depth is that if some weakness is discovered for one protection, then this weakness will hopefully not extend to other layers. For example, if some hacker guesses your password, then this layer of protection is useless. But if the hacker must then pass through firewall rules, then having guessed the password is meaningless.

One can view the entire cyber security industry as being organized around defense in depth. That is, a wide assortment of vendors, suppliers, and other groups actively provide security solutions that are designed to work together. These solutions are generally organized into categories, each of which will be found in most modern cyber defensive set-ups.

You probably try to protect your home PC in this manner, although the truth is that most personal cyber security approaches are ineffective. Perhaps you have a password on your computer, which helps keep intruders away, and perhaps you have some antivirus software running as well. These are weak controls, admittedly, but at least you have a couple of diverse layers of protections.

More extensive defense in depth models exist to help cyber security professionals protect their businesses and organizations. One popular model called AAA, based loosely on a somewhat related scheme invented by security engineers at Cisco Systems, includes the recommendation that three specific layers of defense be included in the protection solution.

The first layer, called *authentication*, is designed to identify who you are, and to then validate this reported identity using a variety of techniques of varying strength. Typing in a password is an example of authenticating one's identity to some system.

The second layer, called *access control*, is designed to ensure that only authorized individuals or groups can have access to a resource such as a file or application. Many different functional methods exist to control access including encryption and firewalls.

The third layer, called *audit*, is designed to support the collection and processing of so-called audit records and logs of activity. Evidence of bad activity can usually be identified in an audit log, and if this evidence is spotted quickly enough, then an attack might be prevented.

Because the cyber security industry is immature, standard means for building a layered defense in depth architecture do not exist. This lies in stark contrast to mature industries such as residential home building, where carpenters are given a standard set of building plans. Cyber security architectures, in contrast, are more ad hoc.

That said, one does encounter familiar sorts of drawings to denote the elements of a security architecture for an enterprise. For example, if some company uses a firewall, an intrusion detection system (IDS), antivirus software, and encryption to protect its assets, then a five-layer security architectural diagram can be constructed to illustrate the resulting gauntlet.

In the diagram below, authorized and unauthorized users would be located to the left of the diagram, attempting access to PC and server assets across an Internet service provider connection. These users would hit the firewall, IDS, password, antivirus, and encryption layers before such access would be allowed. Viewed this way, cyber security architectures perhaps do not look so bad.

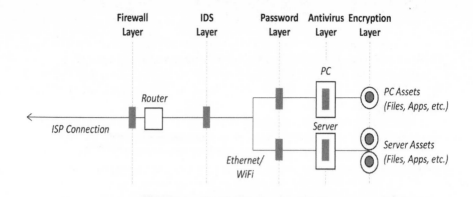

Figure 7-2. Five-Layer Security Architecture for an Enterprise

Most of the chapters throughout the remainder of this book will focus on explaining one or more protective methods that would be included in a layered security architecture. Many of these methods map in an obvious manner to the gauntlet model shown above, but some perhaps do not. It's less important that they fit into a model, than it is for them to provide demonstrable risk reduction for cyber attacks.

To summarize: Defense in depth is a powerful means for organizing security protections into architectures. The theory is that if one layer fails, then hopefully another will pick up the slack. This is not yet fully standardized, but common documentation in the form of architecture diagrams are beginning to emerge slowly in the industry. This is a promising trend.

The next chapter introduces one of the most common and familiar cyber security functional controls that has existed for many years: *Anti-malware software*. Whether you work for a large company or just work at home your personal computer, you are likely familiar with the remaining advantages and obvious disadvantages of this cyber protection method.

8. Anti-Malware Software

Dead birds may be a sign that West Nile virus is circulating between birds and the mosquitoes in an area.

Center for Disease Control (CDC)

A common cyber security tool is the *antivirus* software on your home and work computers. Despite such extensive use, few people have much understanding of how this type of protection works – or at least, how it was intended to work. You will find, sadly, that most antivirus solutions (not all) fall short in reaching their goal of protecting computers from malware.

It's worth noting first that many users are frustrated with antivirus for reasons unrelated to security. Many antivirus products are sold, for example, through Spam-like pop-ups and notifications that confuse buyers and introduce suspicion amongst the credit card-holding public. These are bad business practices, but they have nothing to do with the effectiveness of the typical antivirus method.

The real challenge with antivirus involves a traditional concept known as a *signature*, which is a patterned description of how malware software such as viruses or worms would look on a computer. They are developed by antivirus experts who forensically analyze existing malware and then write out a description that is embedded into antivirus code.

Here's a simple example: Suppose that a virus is detected on the Internet that works by installing a file called Trojan.exe onto Microsoft PCs. When executed, this virus presumably would do something bad, such as popping up a screen asking the user to buy some software on-line. If an expert sees this, then a signature might be developed with the following characteristics:

```
Filename = Trojan.exe
```

This would result in antivirus tools scanning a user's PC to locate and remove anything with filename 'Trojan.exe." While this might sound fine, you might have previously created a *good* file named Trojan.exe that you don't want your antivirus to remove. A new signature would thus need to be created with more specific information such as the virus file's size. Here is how the new signature would look:

```
Filename = Trojan.exe
Size = 125K
```

Assuming your good Trojan.exe file is not also 125K in size, this new signature should at least fix that problem. But suppose the hackers learn what the antivirus tool is now looking for. They will make an adjustment, called a *variant*, that is designed to evade detection. One simple hack is to change the filename to Trojan1.exe. If antivirus experts see this, they must adjust the signature as follows:

```
Filename = Trojan.exe or Trojan1.exe
Size = 125K
```

As you can see, this process has two implications. First, the potential for hackers to continue developing invariants is boundless. That is, the filename can just keep adjusting by incrementing the post-pended number indefinitely (e.g., Trojan235.exe, Trojan236.exe, Trojan237.exe). Second, the challenge of addressing variants results in more signatures with greater complexity.

The cyber security community has thus agreed that signature-based security has clear limitations. In fact, many vendors go out of their way to avoid even using the term to describe any new product they might be developing. The adjective *signature-less* is a popular one across the security community, and this is unlikely to change soon.

But this decision ignores that fact that some types of signatures are quite useful, especially if they focus more on the *behavior* of the software, rather than static, easily changeable characteristics such as a filename. Thus, so-called behavioral analysis has become a popular means for detecting malware on a system, and it usually requires an intimate understanding of malware.

Here's a simple example: One type of malware that is tough to detect is called a *rootkit*. Bad guys build rootkits to embed themselves directly into the memory of your computer, thus blending seamlessly into your operating system in a way that is designed to evade detection. You are not likely to find an obvious filename such as rootkit.exe, for example, if the malware was designed by a skilled developer.

The detection of rootkits thus requires more clever security methods. For instance, rootkits usually enable external access to your operating system for some malicious intruder. One detection measure involves checking for external access to system utilities that do not normally allow incoming such requests. Behavioral anti-malware software would be watching carefully for such situations (see below).

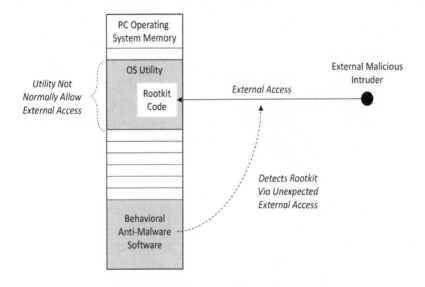

Figure 8-1. Rootkit Detection via Unexpected Access

This behavioral method is based on detecting differences in observed behavior from an expected profile, which is a powerful security approach. Sometimes, when software can detect that a new normal behavioral pattern has emerged, it can dynamically adjust the baseline profile. This type of advanced functionality is called *machine learning*.

Another method for detecting rootkits involves taking a snapshot of a computer's memory and then comparing this to an expected view. As you might guess, with software often being installed and uninstalled on an operating system, meaningful change might not be so easy to highlight. Security experts thus like computers to include a small, high integrity subset of the operating system called a *trusted computing base* or *TCB*.

The power of a TCB is that it allows for a dependable snapshot of a set of trusted operating system utilities that presumably would be stable. By then carefully controlling and monitoring any changes to the TCB, administrators can check to see if malware such as a rootkit has been installed. This is a powerful technique, and one whose use is likely to increase in use in the coming years, especially for mobile devices.

The bottom line with respect to anti-malware tools is that they work to a degree. But the cat-and-mouse game of bad guys developing viruses, followed by the good guys trying to develop solutions, remains tilted in favor of the bad guys. When the bad guys develop something truly new, we call the malware a *zero-day* exploit, because defenders have 'zero days' to have developed a solution.

As you might expect, zero-day exploits are much more frightening if they target critical infrastructure than if they target your home PC. Zero-day attacks on systems such as nuclear power plant safety software, for example, generate considerable anxiety amongst security experts. It is an area in which the community continues to search for solutions.

To summarize: Anti-malware tools are commonly deployed across PCs in home and business. Their signature approach works to a degree, but is easily side-stepped by variants. Behavioral analysis is a more promising approach to detecting malware, but the reality is that hackers will continue to have a big advantage over defenders in malware production.

Our next chapter introduces perhaps the one security solution that is more extensively deployed than anti-malware: *Passwords*. Ironically, despite its leading role in virtually every security solution, passwords suffer from serious shortcomings, and often result in dangerous misconceptions about true levels of security protection in a system.

9. Passwords

Three may keep a secret if two of them are dead.

Benjamin Franklin

The process of typing a *user name* and *password* is the most familiar thing we all do in cyber security. We all use passwords many times per day, and despite what many experts suggest, their use in validating reported identities will not go away any time soon. You will continue to use passwords to watch videos, get your email, buy movie tickets, open Twitter, post to LinkedIn, and on and on.

Passwords are popular because they are convenient. Users love them because they are easy to create, simple to remember, and trivial to reuse across different system and application platforms. In fact, entire families often share one password for on-line services like iTunes or Netflix. As you might guess, such group sharing can have negative security side-effects.

Programmers like passwords because they are easy to integrate across different systems, a property called *interoperability*. If you are creating a web-based service, for example, the functions required to allow entry via user name and password require no new hardware, no new gadgets, and very little programming. Furthermore, no users will ever complain about passwords, because their use is universally accepted.

Cyber security experts refer to passwords use as part of a process known as *authentication*. The textbook definition is that authentication involves using proof factors to validate a reported identity. This validation can be between human beings, computer processes, hardware devices, or any other active entities on a network or system. The general authentication process involves six steps:

Step 1: Identification – In the first step, users supply their name to the system they are trying to access. This is usually a user ID or login name in a format accepted by the system being accessed (e.g., email address, mobile number). Most of the time, user names are not considered secrets. Your email address, for example, is not considered secret in the context of cyber security, because it is easily obtained or viewed.

Step 2: Challenge – The authenticating system then responds by challenging the user to prove their reported name. This is usually a request for a password, but it can be something more involved. Keep in mind that users also authenticate the identity of systems, so this challenge might be someone with a credit card demanding proof that a website is the real merchant it claims to be.

Step 3: Computation – This is an easy step for passwords because it involves the user just remembering or looking something up. For more involved authentication, however, this might involve the user performing a computation, such as solving a math problem. Some early authentication systems included calculator-like devices, where the user would tap in a challenge and then supply the response read from the screen.

Step 4: Response – In this fourth step, the user offers proof to the system that validates the reported identity. As suggested above, this usually involves just typing in a password. Whether the response is offered locally, like on your iPhone, or remotely over a network, will determine how carefully this step is performed. Some authentication solutions go to great lengths to encrypt the response.

Step 5: Validation – This step involves a system checking the validation proof offered to make sure it is as expected. Obviously, for passwords, this is a simple look-up in a table, but more involved protocols might require more processing. It's worth stating that the validation system must be carefully protected from external access to preserve the integrity of the process.

Step 6: Notification – Once the proof has been checked, the system then provides notification of the authentication decision back to the user. This would seem an obvious and trivial step, but keep in mind that incorrect attempts might require notification as well. If enough bad attempts are made, the notification might be that the process has failed and a time-out has been imposed.

These six steps can be represented visually using a simple diagram showing a user Alice trying to authenticate her reported identity to a server Bob. This diagram presumes one challenge and corresponding response. Thus, for scenarios involving multiple proof steps, a technique referred to as *multi-factor authentication*, the process would be repeated for each proof factor.

Figure 9-1. Authentication Process for Alice and Bob

The use of passwords, although familiar and popular, is the weakest form of authentication one might select. Such weakness stems from two issues: First, their sole use is an example of something referred to as *single-factor authentication*. That is, if a hacker manages to break your password protection, then there is no diverse, defense-in-depth protection to fall back on.

The second and more commonly cited weakness with passwords is the relative ease with which bad guys can locate, guess, or figure out the password of some targeted individual or group. Below are some of the ways in which an intruder might determine your password:

Defaults – Many people like to use common, default passwords found frequently across many systems. As you'd expect, the word 'password' is an amazingly popular default setting in many products.

Reuse – If someone knows your password for one system or application, then they might have success trying that password for other systems or applications you use. Sharing and reusing passwords are not recommended.

Guessing – It's often simple to guess someone's password and PIN. Keep in mind that PINs are almost always portions of other well-known number such as home zip code or mobile number.

Cracking – Hackers run programs called *crackers* that target encrypted password files. They often work by encrypting every entry in a dictionary to see if the results match anyone's password.

Phishing – The familiar phony email telling you to "take immediate action to keep such-and-such service working" is an effective means for criminals to trick unsuspecting users into exposing their user IDs and passwords.

More advanced techniques for stealing passwords also exist, and can be much more insidious. One reasonably well-known example involves something called *keystroke monitoring* malware. This type of malware embeds itself into your PC operating system. Such positioning in the path between your keyboard and the process that interprets what you are typing allow the malware to "listen" to your typing.

That is, keystroke monitoring malware collects the keystrokes you type into your keyboard, and exfiltrates the observed activity for review by attackers. Password, credit card numbers, and everything else you type will be thus exposed. Keystroke monitoring software can perform this hack in most cases without users ever knowing that malware was present on the system (see diagram below).

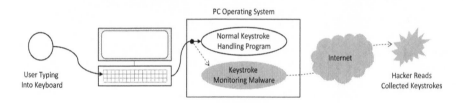

Figure 9-2. Keystroke Monitoring Malware

To summarize: Passwords are the most familiar cyber security control. They are simple and convenient, and no one should expect them to go away soon. They are part of a general process called authentication that allows entities to challenge a reporting identity for proof. Passwords, unfortunately, can be easily guessed, obtained, or tapped.

Despite these challenges, passwords are considered acceptable as a complementary control. When passwords are combined with an additional control, as we will examine in the next chapter, they can provide convenient security, but without creating single points of failure. Passwords are a reasonable component of security solutions, but should not stand alone as a control.

10. Two-Factor Authentication

If you do not have two of the accepted forms of ID, contact the DMV to either obtain a driver's license or ID card and/or contact a passport office.
New Jersey Division of Motor Vehicles

Adding a second factor to the authentication process increases the strength of identity validation considerably. That is, in addition requesting a password, your system or application might demand a second form of proof, not unlike your local motor vehicle agency demanding two forms of ID. Just as with that agency, the result is increased security, albeit at the cost of some additional work.

Two-factor authentication (2FA), as you might expect, is quite popular with security experts. They point to the high likelihood that most cyber attacks will have their root causes somehow related to bad password selection and management. Additionally, two-factor authentication has become significantly easier now that everyone carries around a mobile device.

The most common method for implementing 2FA involves a password and a smart phone. The idea is that some client Alice, who is reporting her identity to some server Bob, would be asked by Bob for proof via a password and response to a mobile text. That is, Bob would ensure that Alice knows her correct password and that she is also in possession of the mobile device on record for her.

Specifically, the four steps for the 2FA scenario involve Bob first requesting a password from Alice, who offers such in the second step. The third step would involve a request for the second factor via a code being sent to Alice's mobile number stored in a database by Bob. When Alice responds with the correct code, as validated by Bob, string authentication has been achieved (see diagram below).

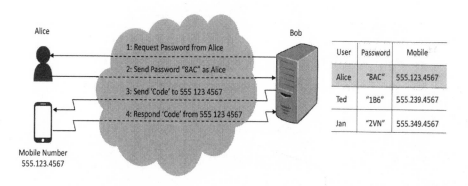

Figure 10-1. Two-Factor Authentication with Password and Mobile

As you might guess, the authenticating system would have to pre-establish the correct password and mobile device number before 2FA can occur. The procedures and supporting systems used to collect and store this registration information are referred to collectively as *authentication infrastructure.* For most companies, this is done by employees in person. For Internet services, it must be done on-line.

An attack known as *spoofing* is directly mitigated by 2FA. Imagine that some attacker Eve wants to gain access to server Bob by impersonating authorized user Alice. Even if Eve has stolen and can supply Alice's password, the 2FA process would demand that she then respond to a text challenge sent via mobile. Unless Eve has also stolen Alice's phone, she won't be able to respond (see diagram below).

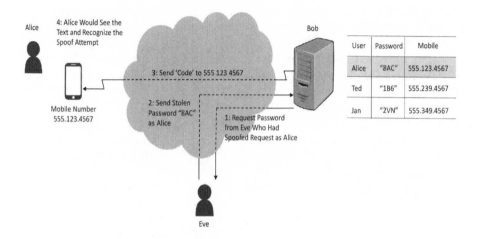

Figure 10-2. Eve's Attempt to Spoof Alice Stopped by 2FA

The 2FA process doesn't have to include passwords and mobiles. That is, it can include any two factors that establish the validity of a reported identity. It works best, however, if these factors use separate communication channels. For example, a password and PIN are similar secrets entered in the same manner. This reduces the strength of the combined check.

Instead, the use of a password or PIN with something different such as a *biometric* test would result in a more diverse, stronger test. In fact, a commonly used 2FA method involves the use of biometric thumbprint tests on smart mobile devices like iPhones to establish an initial factor. This can be followed by an additional factor, such as special embedded cryptographic certificate that identifies the device.

The use of biometrics for 2FA creates interesting possibilities, because human beings have different unique physical attributes to prove identity. These include voice, DNA, thumbprint, and retinal pattern. Such attributes would be encoded digitally and stored using a special mathematical function called a *hash* to represent the pattern in a database.

The security challenge is not that bad guys can reproduce the actual biometric. That is, it's tough for Eve to recreate Alice's real thumbprint for use in the biometric test. Older attacks used gummy bears to try to make a copy of some victim's print, but this method didn't work reliably. Instead, attackers try to subvert biometric registration at the infrastructure level through spoofing.

Keep in mind that when you register your thumbprint, the system must trust that you are binding your real thumb to your real identity. If this is not done in person, then it is possible for someone to hijack your credentials. This underscores the significant challenge that exists in any authentication system to make sure that the underling infrastructure is correct.

This can be illustrated via a four-step process in which Eve's spoofed request to server Bob as Alice is challenged for proof. Assuming Eve has stolen Alice's password, she successfully supplies it to Bob. When Bob then challenges Eve in the third step for Alice's fingerprint, the attack will only succeed if Eve can somehow supply the correct fingerprint pattern, which is clearly not a simple task (see below).

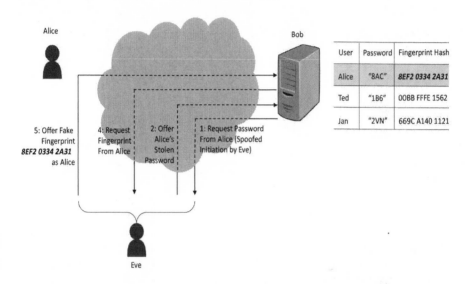

Figure 10-3. Spoofing Registration to Break Biometric Authentication

Several other proof factors exist to support authentication. Location has become a useful complementary factor, although some hackers claim that GPS is easy to spoof. Another popular proof factor involves the motion of the user, perhaps in how a device is held or how one's fingers tend to enter information into a keyboard or display.

These are promising techniques, that when combined, produce an advanced form of authentication called adaptive authentication. It's called adaptive, because it can utilize all available factors to adapt to the situation. If your device, for example, seems to be in an unusual location, then additional authentication might be demanded.

To summarize: Two factor authentication significantly increases the trust one can place in the identity validation process. Mobile texts, biometrics, location, and other factors can be used to established complementary proof, usually with passwords. More advanced adaptive methods show great promise in driving authentication trust to even greater levels.

In the next chapter, we will begin to explore a more traditional form of security, perhaps the longest standing information protection approach know to human beings: *Encryption*. As you will see, while encryption can be complex, if you take your time and try to follow the basics, it can be easily digested and understood by anyone.

Spotlight: Peter Neumann

"If you think cryptography is the answer to your problem, then you don't know what your problems is."

It is generally accepted today that a major component in the cyber security industry involves the collection, organization, and cataloguing of threats, vulnerabilities, and attacks. The origins of this attention to building a proper taxonomy of security issues originated with Peter Neumann, one of the great pioneers in the field of cyber security.

Holding doctorates from both Harvard and Darmstadt, Neumann has spent most of his career at SRI International as a computer scientist. His work there has focused on increasing the trustworthiness, reliability, and dependability of computer systems. He has also been involved in improving the security issues in applications ranging from health care to elections.

Since 1990, Peter has been moderator of a pioneering on-line community sharing network called the ACM Risks Forum (ACM is the Association for Computing Machinery, computer science's longest standing professional society). The Risks Forum pioneered the idea that a large community could share experiences with security, reliability, and trust issues in real, practical systems.

The results of the Risks Forum have been that the security community has come to recognize the great advantage of sharing. By understanding problems that have existed or that currently exist in computer systems, the entire industry benefits. Specifically, by understanding the problems in other systems, designers and operators might prevent similar issues in their own systems.

11. Encryption

Without strong encryption, you will be spied on systematically by lots of people.
Whitfield Diffie

Cryptography involves secret writing between two or more people so that others looking in cannot decipher what's being said or shared. It's the oldest security concept in the world, having been around since people began communicating. The underlying technology of secret writing involves *encryption* and *decryption*, along the lines of the simple Caesar cipher example presented in an earlier chapter.

Cyber security experts define cryptography in terms of five related components that comprise a *cryptosystem*. The idea is that computer systems or applications will need these five components to properly encrypt and decrypt information. The five components of a cryptosystem are as follows:

Encryption Algorithm – This is a scrambling procedure used to create secret writing within a group. It is a function, which implies that if you apply the same encryption function to the same input, you always get the same result.

Decryption Algorithm – This is a descrambling procedure used by members of a group to interpret the secret writing. Decryption can be viewed as the inverse of the encryption function, unraveling the scrambling so that information can be understood.

Set of Keys – This is secret information known by members of the group that parameterize the encryption and decryption. Conventional encryption algorithms use the same keys for encryption and decryption. Public key cryptography is slightly different.

Set of Plaintext – This is the set of readable, understandable text that needs to be protected within the group. The idea is that a recipient of plaintext would not need special knowledge or equipment to understand what is being communicated.

Set of Ciphertext – This is the set of unreadable, secretly written text that cannot be deciphered by members outside the group. Decryption algorithms decode ciphertext into the original, understandable plaintext.

To illustrate the inter-related functions of a cryptosystem, let's examine a simple encryption algorithm based on the binary XOR function. Pronounced *exclusive-OR*, the XOR function works on the binary numbers found in the memory of computers. The operation of XOR is simple: If two binary bits are different, then their XOR result is 1. If they are the same, then the result is 0.

The relevant operations using XOR on binary input to produce binary output are as follows:

(1 XOR 1 = 0), (1 XOR 0 = 1), (0 XOR 1 = 1), and (0 XOR 0 = 0).

Each of these operations is called a bitwise operation because one bit of input produces one bit of output. Mathematicians refer to XOR as a *function* with domain and range equal to the set containing 0 and 1.

XOR can be used to encrypt by calculating the XOR value of binary plaintext with a binary key. The resulting ciphertext is thus hidden from observers, because they do not know the key. If someone does know the key, then this can be used to XOR the ciphertext to obtain the original plaintext. If the plaintext to be encrypted is 0101 1100 and the key is 1010 1010, then here is how the encryption would look:

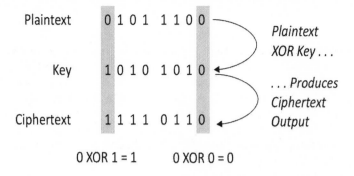

Plaintext   0 1 0 1   1 1 0 0   *Plaintext*
   XOR Key . . .

Key   1 0 1 0   1 0 1 0   *. . . Produces*
   Ciphertext

Ciphertext   1 1 1 1   0 1 1 0   *Output*

0 XOR 1 = 1   0 XOR 0 = 0

For most forms of conventional encryption, the decryption process works by then using the same key used for encryption to also decrypt the ciphertext into the original plaintext. Because this method involves the same key for encryption and decryption, it is called *symmetric encryption*. Here is how such encryption would look for our example:

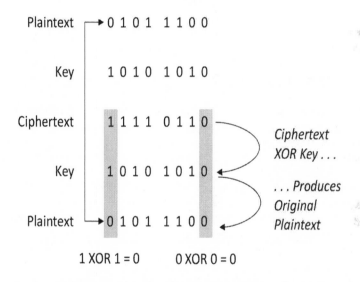

Plaintext   0 1 0 1   1 1 0 0

Key   1 0 1 0   1 0 1 0

Ciphertext   1 1 1 1   0 1 1 0   *Ciphertext*
   XOR Key . . .

Key   1 0 1 0   1 0 1 0   *. . . Produces*
   Original

Plaintext   0 1 0 1   1 1 0 0   *Plaintext*

1 XOR 1 = 0   0 XOR 0 = 0

This process of encrypting information to hide it from unauthorized observers is a powerful means for ensuring secrecy of information such as credit cards being passed across the Internet. It also ensures that information being sent across a network has not been corrupted, simply because the decryption process would not work if any of the plaintext or ciphertext was changed in any way.

The general schema for representing encryption between two *endpoint* entities, designated Alice and Bob, involves the use of an encryption and decryption capability for each endpoint, along with some communication medium, usually the Internet, for sending messages. It's important, obviously, for Alice and Bob to be using the same encryption and decryption functions.

In addition, the general schema for conventional symmetric encryption includes a centralized component called the *key distribution center (KDC)* that provides the secret key to Alice and Bob. A typical KDC will include computing functions and administrative processes administered by people. Obviously, the KDC never expose secret keys to any other endpoint besides Alice and Bob. The schema can be represented as follows:

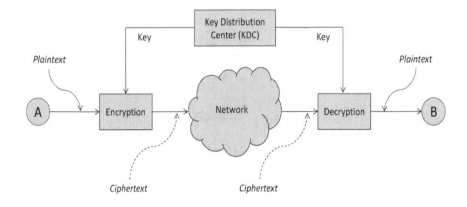

Figure 11-1. Conventional Symmetric Encryption Schema

This conventional symmetric encryption approach is valuable because it enforces two important security properties: First, it allows one endpoint to *authenticate* the reported identity of another. That is, if Alice contacts Bob via encryption using a shared key, then assuming Bob can decrypt and decipher the information sent, he can conclude that only Alice could have initiated this process.

Second, it allows for *secret* communications between Alice and Bob. As we've suggested above, if the KDC is careful to never disclose the shared secret between Alice and Bob, then some unauthorized observer Eve cannot read the information being shared between Alice and Bob. This is a powerful property, one that enables secure e-commerce on the Internet.

To summarize: A conventional cryptosystem is a five-tuple that supports symmetric encryption and decryption of information. The management and handling of cryptographic keys is typically supported by a key distribution center or KDC. Two important security properties, namely authentication and secrecy, are established through conventional encryption schemes.

While these two properties are valuable in computing and networking, a major problem arises with respect to scale. That is, for larger groups of people wanting to authenticate and share secret information, the process of KDC management becomes a huge administrative bottleneck. As a result, a new type of cryptography was invented – and is covered in our next chapter.

12. Public Key Encryption

Only a fool would be excited by the 100th idea, but it might take 100 ideas before one really pays off. Unless you're foolish enough to be continually excited, you won't have the motivation, you won't have the energy to carry it through. God rewards fools.

Martin Hellman

Conventional encryption has the drawback that for large groups, keeping track of adding and deleting keys as the size of the group changes is a challenge. For example, each time a new user is added to a group supporting mutual encryption, a new key must be added for each of the original members. This results in the amount of work to support new users growing much larger as the group size increases.

For example, suppose that two users, A and B, share some key k1, and that adding a new user C introduces the need for two new keys, k2 and k3. Following this logic out to the addition of new users D, E, and F, we can see that the need arises for 12 new keys to be added, resulting in a total of 15 keys supporting six users. The complexity of managing keys in large groups is thus a serious practical issue (see diagram).

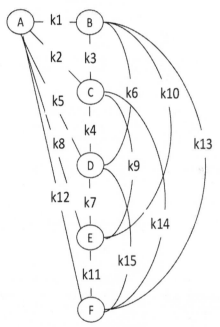

Figure 12-1. Adding Keys in Conventional Encryption

In the mid-1970's, two researchers from Stanford, Whitfield Diffie and Martin Hellman, introduced to the world the idea that keys could be broken into two related components for a special type of encryption. One component would be called the *public key*, and it would be made available to everyone, perhaps in a directory. The second component would be called the *secret key*, and it would be kept private like a password.

The encryption scheme worked like this: Any plaintext encrypted using their special algorithm along with a public key could only be decrypted using the corresponding secret key. Correspondingly, any plaintext encrypted using a secret key could only be decrypted using the corresponding public key. These algorithms and the supporting infrastructure would be referred to collectively as *public key cryptography*.

The most important aspect of their scheme is that individual users would create their own public-secret key pair locally. No centralized key distribution center would be required. Every user would run special software locally that would create unique key pairs, thus removing the need for centralized key administration. Adding a new user would require no immediate action by other users.

A special notation is used to represent this new type of cryptography. It depicts messages as the information requiring cryptographic protection. These messages are then shown to be encrypted using curly braces. Both encryption and decryption use the same curly braces, and they can nest to show repeat operations, such as encrypting and then decrypting a message.

```
{{m}} = m    -- message m encrypted and then decrypted
```

The keys used in the encryption or decryption would be shown as subscripts to the braces. PA and SA, respectively, would be the public and secret keys created and owned by some user A. Thus, we would denote encryption of a message m by user A using public key encryption and its own secret key SA, a process referred to as a *digital signature*, as follows:

$$\{m\}_{SA}$$

Correspondingly, we would denote the decryption of this encrypted message by anyone in possession of PA to the original message m using the corresponding public key PA as follows:

$$\{\{m\}_{SA}\}_{PA} = m$$

As one would expect, we would denote encryption of a message m by anyone in possession of A's public key PA as follows:

$$\{m\}_{PA}$$

Correspondingly, we would denote the decryption of this encrypted message by user A with its secret key SA as follows:

$$\{\{m\}_{PA}\}_{SA} = m$$

These encryption and decryption functions result in a powerful set of properties that have arguably changed the entire world. Amazon.com sells nothing on-line, for example, without this technology. Let's now examine the three most important properties in turn. First, if Alice (A) encrypts a message to Bob (B) using PB, then only Bob can decrypt that message, because he is the only user in possession of SA.

47

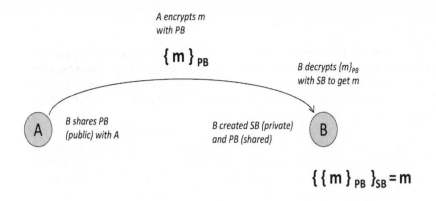

A encrypts m
with PB

$\{ m \}_{PB}$

B decrypts {m}_{PB}
with SB to get m

A

B shares PB
(public) with A

B created SB (private)
and PB (shared)

B

$\{ \{ m \}_{PB} \}_{SB} = m$

Figure 12-2. Ensuring Secrecy from A to B with Public Key Cryptography

This scheme allows credit cards to be sent securely across the Internet to Websites. That is, if A is a user with a browser and credit card, m is the credit card number, and B is a Website, then the exchange of credit card information encrypted with B's public key does not expose the information to anyone on the Internet. This is because only B possesses the secret key to decrypt the card number from A.

Now let's have Alice (A) encrypt a message m to Bob (B) using SA. We can see that Bob, or anyone else in possession of Alice's public key can decrypt the message, but that only Alice could have created it. Remember: Only Alice possesses her secret key, so its use uniquely identifies her. We thus can say that this method establishes authentication of Alice by Bob.

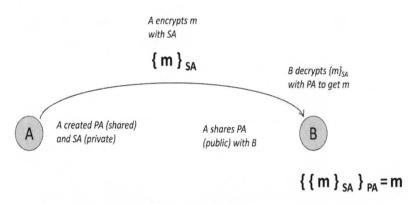

A encrypts m
with SA

$\{ m \}_{SA}$

B decrypts {m}_{SA}
with PA to get m

A

A created PA (shared)
and SA (private)

A shares PA
(public) with B

B

$\{ \{ m \}_{SA} \}_{PA} = m$

Figure 12-3. Authentication of A by B Using Public Key Cryptography

As alluded to earlier, this digital signature scheme allows Alice to authenticate to Bob, but would be a terrible choice for sending credit card numbers, because anyone on the Internet could decrypt the message and steal the card number. Unfortunately, the first protocol above ensured secrecy, and the second ensured authentication, but neither did both.

To rectify this situation, a new protocol can be followed that accomplishes both security objectives. It does this via encryption by Alice first using SA for authenticity and then using PB for secrecy. Bob then decrypts the received ciphertext with SB to unlock the secrecy and then PA to check the authenticity of Alice. It's quite a clever scheme and it looks as follows:

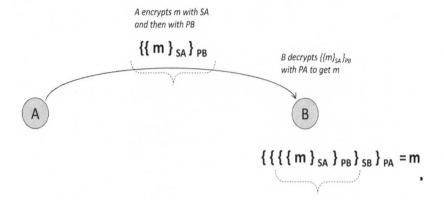

Figure 12-4. Secrecy and Authentication in the Same Protocol

One remaining challenge is that conventional, symmetric cryptography was originally designed to handle large chunks of data efficiently. For example, encrypting a large file would be best done using conventional cryptographic algorithms with a single key. As we described earlier, however, this creates key distribution and management scaling problems for larger groups.

Whit Diffie and Martin Hellman came up with an ingenious solution which is called *Diffie-Hellman Key Exchange*. Their proposal is that the message m encrypted for secrecy and authentication, should be a conventional key used for symmetric encryption between Alice and Bob. This amazing insight allows for conventional crypto without the need for a key distribution center.

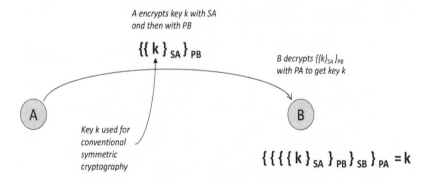

Figure 12-5. Diffie-Hellman Key Exchange

This landmark protocol by Diffie and Hellman earned them the highest award in the Computer Science Community: The Turing Award, named after Alan Turing, the pioneer computer scientist. Many believe that Diffie-Hellman Key Exchange is the finest cyber security contribution ever to the scientific, technical community. One can certainly make the case for this view.

To summarize: Public key cryptography removes the need for centralized key distribution centers. It supports secrecy and authentication properties by using public and private key encryption and decryption. Diffie-Hellman Key Exchange allows the use of public key cryptography to support existing symmetric algorithms that are optimized for bulk encryption.

The implications of this new security technology have been felt most directly in *secure e-commerce*. That is, the entire on-line global marketplace has been enabled by public key cryptography, and we examine this critical application of cyber security technology in our next chapter.

13. Secure E-Commerce

A very large percentage of economic activity is shifting online and it makes sense that there are more services that are going to charge. It also means there are going to be more people willing to pay.

Marc Andreesen

Public key cryptography has had a profound global societal influence by enabling the secure sale of goods and services on the Internet. Customers with browsers wanting to purchase items from on-line stores such as Amazon.com are typically concerned with sending credit card numbers across the Internet. The use of cryptography, coupled with ingenious decisions by browser vendors solves this challenge.

The way it works is simple: Third-party business entities called *certification authorities* or *CAs* create their own public and secret key pairs that are used to oversee the secure e-commerce process. What they do is invite commerce vendors with websites to send over their own public key – for a fee. The CA then sends back a so-called *signed certificate* that vouches for the fact that it was truly *that* website's public key that was received and is included in the certificate.

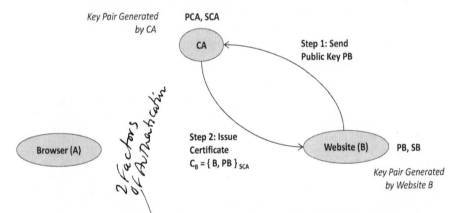

Figure 13-1. Website Public Key Vouched in a Signed Certificate from a CA

Vouching for the public key of a website using a certificate requires that the CA perform authentication. This can be done weakly using email checks on sending domains. It can also be done more thoroughly using 2FA, perhaps including a mobile code. Alternatively, it can be done in the strongest sense using in-person, face-to-face attestation. These options are called *assurance levels.*

Once the website has its certificate, user browsers can obtain the website's public key via the certificate. The protocol used for this exchange is called *secure sockets layer* or *SSL*, and it was introduced by experts at Netscape, led by Marc Andreesen. After the exchange, the browser possesses the certificate, which includes, among other administrative items, the name of the website and its public key. The certificate is encrypted with the secret key of the CA.

The challenge is how the browser can decrypt this without having to make requests to the CA for its public key. The solution introduced by Netscape in the mid-1990's involved embedding the public keys of all CAs into the actual browser code. This way, users only need to download a browser to obtain the public keys of all CAs signing website certificates. It allows the browser to decrypt the certificate to obtain the public key, which is then used to encrypt credit cards (see below).

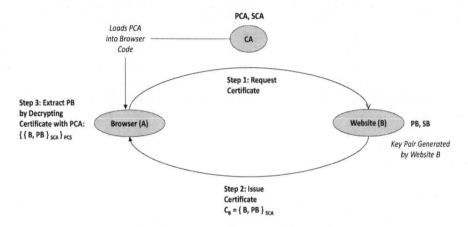

Figure 13-2. Decrypting Certificates on the Browser to Obtain Public Keys

An initial concern with secure e-commerce on the Internet is that users must trust that their sensitive credit card information is not mishandled by the website offering them goods. This is a familiar concern to anyone who ever used a credit card, but the Internet makes this information so much more accessible to hackers around the world.

A second concern is that users must trust that the CA has created a valid certificate for a given website. If, for example, the CA has been compromised and a forged certificate finds its way onto browsers, then the possibility arises for phony commerce sites to be set up with certificates that will properly resolve in the browser. This type of forgery has occurred several times, and is a new, invisible type of hack that on-line users should recognize.

To summarize: The use of public key cryptography and certificates, in the context of trust assurance from certificate authorities, is a promising area of cyber security. It is an area, for instance, that enables secure e-commerce, as well as other promising new applications for elections, financial services, gaming, and on and on. Young people learning cyber security at the university level are typically drawn to this area because of the creative possibilities that exist for new applications.

In our next chapter, we will shift gears somewhat, with the introduction of the basics of the underlying language of the Internet, known as TCP/IP. All new Internet-based technology is built in the context of TCP/IP, so anyone learning cyber security must understand the basics of this protocol suite. In fact, one could make the case that TCP/IP is to cyber security as the periodic table is to chemistry.

14. TCP/IP Overview for Security

A decision was made long ago about the size of an IP address – 32 bits. At the time, it was a number much larger than anyone could imagine ever having that many computers, but it turned out to be too small.

Jon Postel

To understand cyber security, you need to first understand the underlying language of the Internet known as the *Internet protocol* or *IP*. Two computers communicate over IP using five pieces of data: The addresses of each computer, the numbered ports of the programs running on each computer, and the higher-level protocol, usually the Transport Control Protocol (TCP), being used in conjunction with IP.

Here's an example: If you browse a website on the Internet, then TCP will coordinate the IP session. Your browser will first grab a local port number from your computer's operating system and the website administrator will have already assigned port 80 to its web server software. Your computer and the website computer will both have IP addresses, which are the logical equivalent of physical street addresses. The resulting five pieces of information – two IP addresses, two port numbers, and TCP – are collectively referred to as a *five-tuple*.

IP addresses are usually assigned dynamically by the Internet Service Provider (ISP) to the user with a browser, often referred to as a *client*. IP addresses are usually assigned in a more static manner by the local network administrator for the website, often referred to as a *server*. The resulting IP interaction is called a *client-server* protocol. This is relevant to cyber security, because protection devices such as *firewalls* must ensure that the interaction follows security rules. Five-tuples are illustrated in the diagram below:

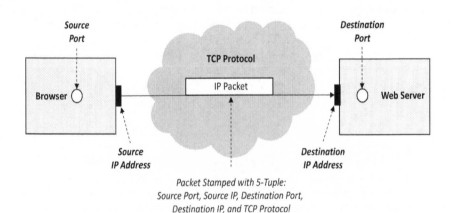

Packet Stamped with 5-Tuple:
Source Port, Source IP, Destination Port,
Destination IP, and TCP Protocol

Figure 14-1. Five-Tuple Information in a Browsing Session

It is important to understand, from a cyber security perspective, that the two endpoints, referred to generically as Alice (A) and Bob (B), can misrepresent their source IP address or source port information. That is, the local administrator of each machine, or anyone with sufficient access to each machine, can craft packets that have whatever source information is desired.

This ability to lie about Internet packets should come as no major surprise, because most people recognize that you can write down a fake *from-address* on a physical postal envelope without too much difficulty. Obviously, you would have problems if the sent letter needed to be returned, and you would also have truly obvious problems if the *to-address* was incorrect. The diagram below illustrates some of the spoofing options and corresponding implications for TCP sessions:

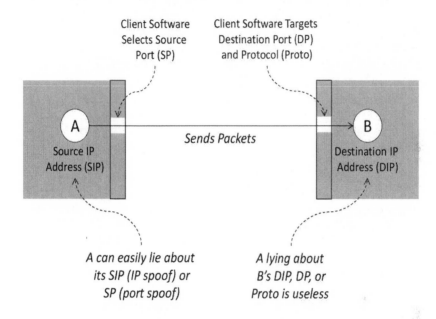

Figure 14-2. Another View of the TCP Process

TCP coordinates the back-and-forth communication between browsers and websites by alternating who is the *source* and who is the *destination* of information being sent. Information is sent over IP using data called *packets*, which come with a header and a content field. The header is like the outside of a paper envelope and the content is like what you put inside the envelope.

In order that your browser, or any other program using TCP over the Internet, can gain access to the website, it must go through a three-step handshake managed by TCP. Each step in the handshake is intended to supply the corresponding entity with the address and port information it needs to proceed. Each step also includes a *sequence number*, which is used to help sort out the ordering of the sent and received packets.

The first packet from your browser to the website is called a SYN packet. It's like the first knock on the door from your browser telling the website that someone wants to browse. The SYN packet has the source IP address of your computer, most likely issued by your Internet Service Provider (ISP), and targets the destination IP address of the website. The header of the packet designates that it is a SYN by setting a specific SYN bit to be 1.

The second packet from the website back to the browser is called a SYN/ACK. It's like the response to the browser's initial knock, and it reverses the source and destination IP addresses, as well as the port numbers. Like the SYN packet, the header designates that it is a SYN/ACK by setting both SYN and ACK to be 1. It is important to see that the SYN packet has ACK = 0, but the SYN/ACK, and all subsequent packets will have ACK = 1. More on this important point below.

The third packet is a response back from the browser to the website and is called an ACK. It is issued from the source IP address of the browser to the destination IP address of the website, running software on TCP port 80. Once this has been received by the website, you are now ready to send and receive data, video, images, and other content with the site. Figure 14-3 illustrates the three-step TCP set-up and corresponding ACK values:

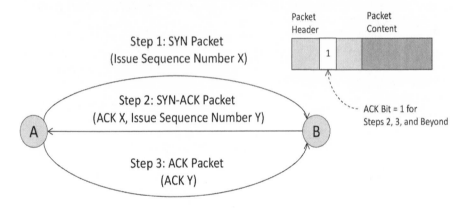

Figure 14-3. Three-Step TCP Handshake Between Client Browser and Website

This so-called *TCP/IP handshake* provides the base communication on which most network security methods operate. The most common security method, known as a firewall, sits between clients and servers, and has the obligation to determine what should be allowed and what should be blocked. This is done based on locally defined security policies.

To summarize: The communication plumbing of the Internet is based on the TCP/IP family of protocols. It involves packets being sent between communicating entities, which implies that security protections for the Internet are likely to require integration with these steps of TCP/IP. The initial SYN packet is one of the most important factors in such security integration.

As we will see in the next chapter, policy-based decisions by special security devices called *firewalls* will depend on many different factors, but one of the most important of these factors is the simple ACK bit in the TCP handshake. That simple bit turns out to play a powerful role in protecting Internet resources from being accessed by unauthorized individuals.

15. Firewalls

*Each portion of a building separated by one or more firewalls that comply with
the provisions of this section shall be considered a separate building.*
Section 705 of the NJ Building Code

Firewalls are devices that monitor and control network traffic based on a set of rules in a
defined *security policy*. Firewalls serve as filters to allow or block requests from users for
services. The most common deployment of a firewall involves protecting the inbound and
outbound services for an organization. This typically includes web services, email, remote
access, cloud file storage, and on and on.

The owner of a firewall is usually defined organizationally. That is, if you are part of
a company, then some member of the corporate security group will deploy and run a
firewall on behalf of the entire employee pool. They will define policies consistent with the
culture and norms of the group. Media companies, for example, will likely have more liberal
access policies than conservative financial institutions.

The operation of a firewall follows a simple process in which packets from an
originating source such as a user are sent to a destination such as a server. The packets find
their way via a network connection to an inserted firewall that inspects each packet and
decides whether to allow or deny the packet continued passage along to the server. It's that
simple (see below).

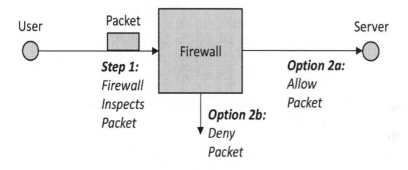

Figure 15-1. Basic Firewall Scheme

To understand how firewalls work more generally, let's start with some entity A trying to
connect via TCP/IP to another entity B. As we learned in the last chapter, we know that the
first packet sent from A to B will be a SYN packet with the ACK bit set to 0. Since all
subsequent packets will have the ACK bit set to 1, we can use this hint to detect the first
packet in a session request.

Furthermore, since the initial packet will include the destination IP address for the
system being targeted, as well as the destination port of the service being requested, the
firewall can make its allow or deny decision accordingly. Destination ports for Internet
services are established based on an agreed-to numbering scheme. Web servers run on
port 80, email servers on port 25, and so on.

If the firewall sees that the ACK bit is 0, and that the requested destination port (DP) is considered acceptable, as perhaps with web services on port 80, then the packet will be allowed to proceed. If, however, the DP is not considered acceptable, as perhaps with email services on port 25, then the packet will be dropped.

Any firewall operating on collected packets in this manner is referred to as a *packet filter*. Many routers include packet filtering in their operation, but usually the function is supported by a firewall product that is obtained and installed specifically for security. Firewalls include much more advanced features, but the core protection is performed on a packet-by-packet basis.

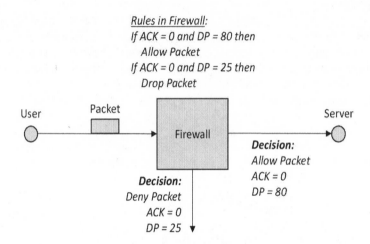

Figure 15-2. Packet Filter

The rules for enforcing an organization's desired security policy are encoded into the firewall by local administrators. If, for example, the local team decides to prevent outbound web surfing, then the firewall would include a specific rule to stop this. In this case, it would look for and then *drop* any packet being sent over TCP that had an external IP address and a destination port of 80.

Embedded in the firewall would be a rule that defines the desired action for a given set of conditions. Thus, for the example above, a rule would be included that would prevent outbound web surfing via a simple table. The elements of the table include values to be matched in the packet header. If all the elements match the specified value, then the associated action would be performed.

The web surfing prevention rule would look to drop any TCP packet with the ACK bit set to 0 that is coming from an internal IP address on some arbitrary port that is being sent to any external IP address on port 80. This is represented in tabular form associating each variable with the value that must match for the corresponding action to occur.

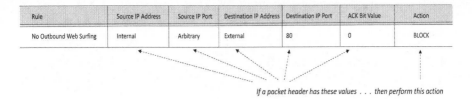

Rule	Source IP Address	Source IP Port	Destination IP Address	Destination IP Port	ACK Bit Value	Action
No Outbound Web Surfing	Internal	Arbitrary	External	80	0	BLOCK

If a packet header has these values . . . then perform this action

Figure 15-3. Sample Firewall BLOCK Rule in Tabular Form

The example above shows that if a given packet matches the specified values for each of the information variables in the table, then the corresponding block action would be taken. In practice, a graphical user interface would be used for this tabular information. That is, a security administrator would just point and click on values to set up or modify firewall rules.

A strategy often used by firewall administrators involves something called *default block*. This involves including a default rule that will perform a block action on any packet that is not specifically designated to be allowed. The idea is to require that the firewall administrator list the allowable services, rather than list the blocked services.

Firewalls implementing *default block* policies reduce the overall number of rules in a security policy, because there are almost always fewer services to be allowed than prevented. Each allowed service, however, requires more firewall rules, because each of the packets in the TCP handshake for a given service must be explicitly permitted by the firewall.

To illustrate, let's assume that a given organization wants to permit web surfing out of the enterprise to the Internet, but to block every other service. The corresponding rules must allow the first SYN packet, the second SYN/ACK packet, and then the third ACK packet. The corresponding rules, with the *default block* policy are shown in the table below (with * designating an arbitrary value that always matches).

Rule	Source IP Address	Source IP Port	Destination IP Address	Destination IP Port	ACK Bit Value	Action
Outbound Web Surf – SYN	Internal	*	External	80	0	ALLOW
Outbound Web Surf – SYN/ACK	External	80	Internal	*	1	ALLOW
Outbound Web Surf – ACK	Internal	*	External	80	1	ALLOW
Default Block	*	*	*	*	*	BLOCK

Figure 15-4. Sample Firewall ALLOW Rules in Tabular Form

Upon closer inspection, notice that the first and third rules in the above tabular form are different only in the ACK bit value. This implies that if all else is equal, then regardless of whether the ACK bit is 0 or 1, the allow action will be taken. For this reason, professional firewall administrators would combine these two rules into one combined rule as shown below.

Rule	Source IP Address	Source IP Port	Destination IP Address	Destination IP Port	ACK Bit Value	Action
Outbound Web Surf – SYN or ACK	Internal	*	External	80	*	ALLOW
Outbound Web Surf – SYN/ACK	External	80	Internal	*	1	ALLOW
Default Block	*	*	*	*	*	BLOCK

Figure 15-5. Sample Optimized Firewall ALLOW Rules

The example shown is obviously just for one service, namely, web surfing. For an organization to allow a full range of services, corresponding firewall rules would be added carefully to the firewall, with the *default block* rule always being appended at the end. The process of constructing firewall rules is laborious, but most would agree that the effort is well worth the trouble.

To summarize: Firewalls support allowing or denying access to requested resources based on policy. As one might expect, the simple examples shown above are more complex in non-trivial network settings. In addition, much more advanced capabilities are found in the enterprise so that firewall decisions can be made based on more involved factors than just five-tuple information.

Now that we've covered a bit of TCP/IP and the use of firewalls to inspect packets, let's digress further into an area of cyber security that uses protocols to find systems on a network, and to then determine some reasonable next step. Such steps range from updating inventory lists to performing full-out hacking on the discovered system. This general discovery technique is called *scanning*.

Spotlight: Robert Morris Sr.

"The notion that we are raising a generation of children so technically sophisticated that they can outwit the best efforts of the security specialists of America's largest corporations and the military is utter nonsense."

Just about every cyber security control in modern applications, operating systems, and networks traces its roots to the earliest protections designed into the Unix operating system nearly half a century ago. While many different Bell Labs contributors offered creative assistance to these pioneering security features, no one had more prolific contributions than Robert Morris Sr.

After studying mathematics at Harvard, Bob joined Bell Labs in 1960, and quickly began work on a new operating system called Multics. Sensing that Multics seemed too complicated, the Bell Labs group developed a simpler version with a simpler name called Unix. It was this project and the resultant operating system that would support Bob's greatest contributions to computing and to information security.

One of his most well-known early developments was a program called crypt that was used to encipher password files on Unix. This technique seems obvious today, but at the time it was a clever means for preventing attacks that hadn't even materialized. This technique of adding security before a crisis emerges is something we can all learn from today.

After retiring from Bell Labs in 1986, Bob accepted a position at the National Security Agency, serving as a senior scientist in the newly formed National Computer Security Center. During his short tenure in government, he helped the NCSC develop a series of useful standards for developing and operating secure computer systems and networks.

16. Scanning

Computer security helps ensure that your computers, networks, and peripherals work as expected all the time.

Bruce Schneier

A popular security technique involves using a software tool called a *scanner* that attempts to connect with target systems or networks across a TCP/IP connection to see what it can find. As you might imagine, if you run a scanner on a company network, you will find all sorts of interesting things, including many systems you might not have expected would be present.

To support scanning, the security team must first position the scanner in one of three places that will make sense for the desired purpose. The scanner can be embedded in the operating system of some computer, from which it can run scans on the applications present on that system. Administrators would assign proper privileges to the scanner so that it can reach whatever is of interest.

A second positioning would be on a corporate network, sometimes referred to as an *Intranet* or enterprise network. By running a scan from this vantage point, the security team can find and better understand what sort of systems and applications are running inside the company. Again, this often results in locating systems that no one expected to find.

The third positioning for a scanner is the public Internet or any network outside the private confines of an enterprise. This type of scanning is particularly powerful because it accurately simulates the experience of an external hacker with no special privileges in the enterprise. Scanning from the Internet also allows for a more holistic view of any cloud services that enterprise might be using. The three scanning options are depicted below in Figure 16-1.

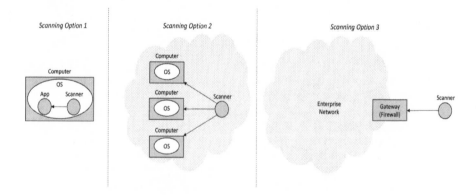

Figure 16-1. Positioning Options for Scanning

The detailed interaction a scanner has with a target entity involves one of three different actions. First, it might simply send a single SYN packet to see if a SYN/ACK response is obtained. If the packet response is obtained, the scanner then simply stops the interaction to avoid any further detection or logging. This is called a *half-scan*, because it only goes halfway to establishing a real connection.

The second interaction would involve a scanner establishing a full TCP/IP connection by responding to the SYN/ACK packet. The resulting *full scan* allows the scanner to observe the response behavior of the targeted system more closely, albeit probably under log surveillance. Sometimes useful hints about the software being used by the target system can be obtained through the less stealth analysis.

The third interaction would involve not just establishing the full connection, but doing something called a *deep scan*. Such an approach would involve using the established session access to look around, probe directories, and try to build an understanding of exactly what is running and available in the target system. More determined hackers generally follow this path. These three types of scans are depicted in Figure 16-2.

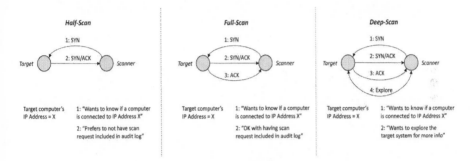

Figure 16-2. Half, Full, and Deep Scans

You might be wondering whether scanning could also provide malicious hackers with similar information about target systems. This is, in fact, one of the paradoxes of scanners. They can be used as helpful tools for security administrators with benign motivation, or they can be used by malicious actors to obtain information about a system being considered for subsequent hacking.

Back in the 1990's a popular scanner was developed by Dan Farmer and Wietse Venema, two pioneers of network security. Their tool helped system and network administrators detect vulnerabilities in targeted systems and became quite popular across the world. As a bit of a joke, they allowed users to set up and name the tool SANTA, if done for good purposes, or SATAN if done for bad.

When scanners are used for hacking, the malicious actor would not perform the scan from a source address or account that can be detected by security teams or law enforcement. What they would do instead is hack an intermediary system, from which scans would then be performed. This way, when full or deep scans are run from the intermediary, any mitigation would not affect the originating hacker.

The use of intermediaries is a powerful point because it helps explain why hack-backs are poor policy for cyber security teams or governments. When a hack produces consequence to some target, it is almost certainly performed from an unsuspecting, intermediary system. Thus, a hack-back might cause damage to an innocent intermediary such as a home PC or other innocent system.

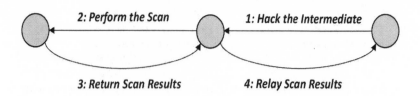

2: Perform the Scan   1: Hack the Intermediate

3: Return Scan Results   4: Relay Scan Results

Figure 16-3. Intermediary System Used for Malicious Scanning

Cyber security experts typically warn policy makers that scans can go only *so far* in establishing useful information about target systems. Some inexperienced observers wrongly assume that a scan means a full analysis of security with corresponding actions taken to wipe clean any problems. Unfortunately, as you can see now, scans are nowhere near as thorough.

To summarize: scans can be done for applications, systems, or entire networks. They can be performed in a half, full, or deep scan mode, depending on the motivation. They can also be performed for benign discovery and understanding of a given system, or they can be used as a component of a malicious hack, usually employing unsuspecting intermediaries to help hide the source of the scan.

In the next chapter, we introduce a security technique that complements firewalls and scanners. It is a technique that attempts to "watch" system or network activity to determine if something unusual or suspicious might be occurring. This technique is called *intrusion detection*, and it is one of the most commonly found security controls in any company.

17. Intrusion Detection

A model of a real-time intrusion-detection expert system capable of detecting break-ins, penetrations, and other forms of computer abuse is described.
Dorothy Denning

Just as firewalls make decisions to block or allow TCP/IP services based on a set of security policy rules, complementary security devices called *intrusion detection systems (IDS)* monitor computing activity to detect evidence of cyber attacks. An IDS is often placed next to the firewall in a typical enterprise or network because this is usually an excellent place to search for attack indicators.

Two methods can be used in an IDS: The first method involves collecting information on a network to detect evidence of attacks. This approach requires the ability to collect traffic in real-time as well as the ability to compare this traffic against rules that describe the steps of an attack. This often requires storage of information about the state of the attack as it progresses.

A simple example involves an IDS watching for password guessing on a network. Its functionality would require a simple detection function with a counter. Thus, if the IDS detects an invalid password message to some external user, then it will take note and then keep watching. If additional invalid passwords occur, perhaps three total, then the IDS might send an alarm to a security server (see below).

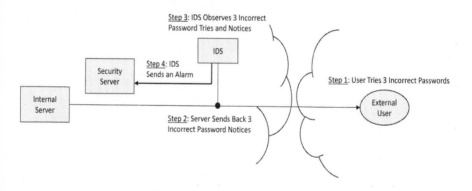

Figure 17-1. Password Guessing IDS

A difference between firewall and IDS methods is the degree to which an IDS can maintain so-called *state* information. This involves the IDS keeping track of indicators as a system changes its state over time. As should be evident from the password guessing algorithm shown above, detecting the attack requires that the IDS count the number of guesses over time.

The specific description of a given attack is known as a *signature*, and most IDS approaches base their alarm generation on matching what is observed with what has been described in a signature. For example, we just illustrated the signature that three or more incorrect password guesses over a short duration denote a possible attack. Signatures have their respective pros and cons.

First, it should be obvious that *false positives* can occur easily with common signatures. For example, getting your password wrong three times in a row might be innocent and easily explainable in many different cases. Users forget passwords all the time, so drawing the conclusion that this indicates a cyber security attack might be incorrect – hence, the false positive.

Second, attackers can easily side-step signatures by adjusting their behavior sufficiently to avoid detection by the IDS. For example, if the password guessing signature defines the period of analysis for guessing to be one minute, then the attacker can create a so-called *variant* attack that proceeds more slowly to avoid detection within the one minute duration.

The diagram below shows time progressing downward with three attack steps – password guesses, specifically – being made outside the one-minute duration, which ensures that the attack will in fact evade the defined signature:

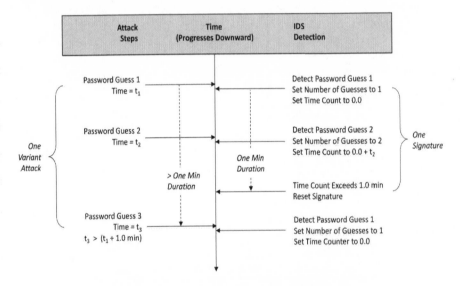

Figure 17-2. Password Guessing Variant to Avoid IDS Signature

Most IDS techniques are designed to examine traffic at a network gateway to identify anomalies. An alternate, and more traditional approach to IDS involves sifting through the data in an audit log to highlight evidence that an attack might be occurring. This technique is often performed after-the-fact on recorded activity records, rather than on-the-fly for network IDS.

The algorithms for audit log analysis are like the signature methods in the IDS examples we've looked at above. That is, a description of normal activity is compared with the evidence in the log file of what has occurred on the target system. One advantage of audit log analysis, however, is that certain types of signature weaknesses, such as time management, might be addressed.

Take the password guessing example shown above. Rather than work from one-minute signature intervals to detect the guessing, log analysis can search more holistically through the entire set of records. Algorithms that perform statistical analysis over a longer period might uncover the low and slow nature of certain attack variants (see diagram below).

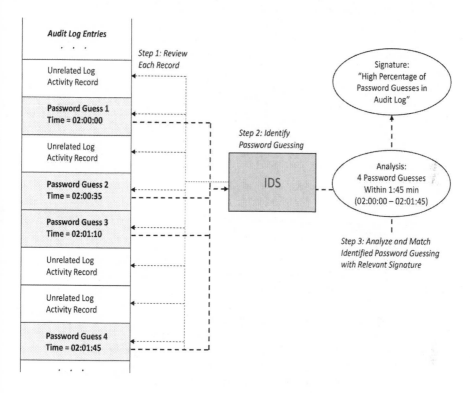

Figure 17-3. Detecting Variants through Log Analysis

The disadvantage of after-the-fact analysis is that it takes time for completion, and might not identify a given attack quickly enough to prevent serious consequence. The advantage, however, is that such analysis can be more comprehensive than on-the-fly methods, and can support a more rigorous study of the true nature of an attack. In the end, both types of IDS are recommended.

More recent IDS tools have been designed based on a new method that includes live mitigation of a detected intrusion. Generally included in network-based, on-the-fly IDS, the resultant capability, called an *intrusion prevention system* (IPS), uses the detection of an attack indicator as the first step, and then follows up with some security action designed to reduce risk.

The most popular IPS function involves something called a *source IP address shun*. What happens here is that the IPS first detects that hacking seems to be occurring from some identified source, usually so-designated by its IP address. The IPS then creates a local rule that will look for subsequent activity from that source IP address to specifically block or *shun* such action (see below).

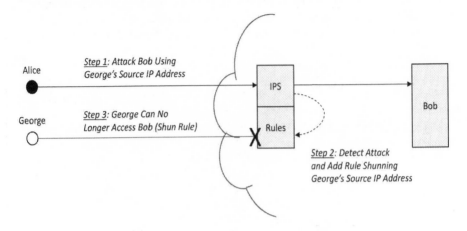

Figure 17-4. IPS Shun of Offending Source IP Address

While the shun capability of an IPS would seem desirable, even essential for a cyber security architecture, it does come with serious drawbacks. The most obvious is that an offender can lie about its source IP address. That is, Alice can attack Bob, using the spoofed source IP address of some unsuspecting George. The IPS would then shun George, and the result is that a potentially authorized user would be blocked.

The typical modern enterprise security architecture will use IPS only sparingly. A common approach is to purchase an IPS with its mitigation capability in place if needed, but to run the IPS in a passive mode. That is, by just inspecting traffic and providing alarms to the security team, a passive mode IPS is nothing more than a traditional IDS.

To summarize: Intrusion detection systems complement firewalls and scanning by searching for attack indicators based on signatures. A major goal of an IDS is to reduce the number of false positive alarms, but this is not always easy. An intrusion prevention system introduces the possibility that after detecting an indicator, a security mitigation step can be taken.

In the next chapter, we introduce a special type of IDS called *data leakage prevention* or *DLP*. This security tool is focused on searching for evidence that sensitive data is being leaked from the enterprise. As you might expect, in the current climate of sensitive data breaches, DLP systems play a critical role in protecting the enterprise.

18. Data Leakage Prevention

A small leak can sink a great ship.

Benjamin Franklin

The problem of *data leakage* from an enterprise to the Internet or some other untrusted network is a familiar discussion point in cyber security. Leaks have been occurring for as long as organizations have had secrets to keep, but computers and networks have increased both the volume of secrets, and how such secrets can be shared with unauthorized individuals or groups.

Data leakage involves a company insider leaking proprietary or even classified information to an outsider. This could be a noble act, as in the case of a whistle-blower in the presence of illegal or immoral activity, but more often it is nefarious, as in a criminal selling company secrets to an interested party such as a competitor.

Leaks can be arranged into a simple taxonomy, as shown in Figure 18-1 below, using a two-by-two matrix. The rows of the matrix designate whether the leak is intentional or accidental, and the columns designate whether the leak uses officially sanctioned organizational computers and networks, or separate privately owned systems such as your home PC.

	Inadvertent	**Deliberate**
Official IT	*Someone accidentally releasing sensitive data using company systems*	*Someone intentionally releasing sensitive data using company systems*
Shadow IT	*Someone accidentally releasing sensitive data using non-company systems*	*Someone intentionally releasing sensitive data using non-company systems*

Figure 18-1. Taxonomy of Leakage Cases

The use of private infrastructure is a challenge in industrial cyber security. That is, when employees use their own Gmail accounts for email, Box account for storage, and Facebook accounts for communication, the enterprise security team loses control of the associated data. For this reason, such private usage is referred to as *shadow IT*.

The solution to this problem, called *data leakage prevention*, involves so-called DLP tools that are programmed to detect patterns in data being passed across corporate gateways to external networks. For example, if sensitive information in company XYZ is marked "XYZ-Sensitive," then the DLP system would be programmed to detect that pattern.

Obviously, this approach will work effectively for inadvertent data leakage, which would involve senders not stripping the sensitive markings. Malicious leakers, on the other hand, would condition the data to avoid DLP detection. This makes the baseline approach less useful for detecting malicious leakage, but nonetheless important to stop accidental leaks.

The algorithms used for DLP systems treat data as a series of strings, which are sequences of characters, usually separated by spaces, periods, tabs, and other delimiters. The specific pattern matching is usually done based on the following techniques:

Direct String Match – This involves company-specific definition of locally relevant string patterns such as 'secret' or 'proprietary.' If data passes across a DLP system that is programmed to look for these patterns, then the traffic would either be stopped or would trigger an alert.

Variable String Match – This involves patterns that cannot be directly coded into a strong match. Detecting social security numbers, for example, requires a match that uses variables to depict patterns. Thus, the DLP system would look for social security numbers arranged as follows: '$n_1 n_2 n_3 - n_4 n_5 - n_6 n_7 n_8 n_9$,' where each variable n_i is a number from 0 to 9.

Regular Expression Match – This involves using a mathematical language that can describe repeat patterns. Regular expressions describe a set of strings in a clever manner, using a defined syntax developed decades ago. For example, the regular expression *.txt defines all strings that end with 'txt.'

More advanced methods for data leakage prevention focus on behavioral patterns of users. That is, in addition to using known patterns, modern DLP systems also observe user behavior for evidence that data might be leaked. This might include clever methods such as watching for increased connections to external social networks, perhaps as part of a leakage process or campaign.

The architectural options for DLP include two choices. DLP systems can be deployed at natural chokepoints on a network. This places DLP systems at the perimeter or demilitarized zone (DMZ) portion of a network. Alternatively, they can be positioned on endpoint systems to watch for local actions such as copying data from a PC to a memory stick.

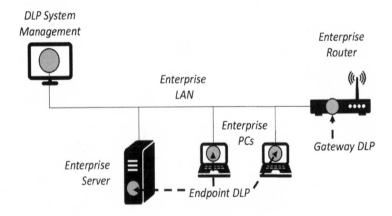

Figure 18-2. Architectural Positioning of DLP Systems in an Enterprise

Endpoint DLP solutions must be carefully managed, because they can easily push employees to shadow IT. For example, if an employee working from home wants to use a personal printer for work-related material, then this often requires transfer to a personal account. If DLP restricts this transfer, then the employee might just create and manage the data outside the control of the security team.

To summarize: Data leakage prevention tools are special types of intrusion detection systems that are focused on preventing accidental and deliberate leaks of data from insiders to outsiders. DLP systems use several detection approaches to try to identify leaks. Usually, DLP systems are positions at network gateways or on system endpoints.

In the next chapter, we look at a special type of process that helps organizations obtain and share information that can lead to improved signatures. Such threat information sharing should be viewed as an essential means by which firewalls, intrusion detection systems, data leakage systems, and other security tools are operated using the best available threat data.

19. Threat Information Sharing

Information is not knowledge.

Albert Einstein

An important discipline in cyber security involves the *threat information sharing* between entities. These entities can be human beings, perhaps working in different organizations, offering useful tips about how a given cyber attack might be spotted. But they can also be machines, perhaps connected across the Internet, passing attack-related information back and forth using automated protocols.

In either case, whether human or automated, the sharing of information lends to most people's common sense about how an attack might be stopped. For example, if one bank sees an attack targeting their financial systems, then it stands to reason that by sharing this information with other banks, everyone ultimately benefits, so long as the sharing is balanced on common footing.

Vendors have recently emerged that provide *threat feed* services to corporate customers based on all-source research across the Internet. These feeds generally combine both human and automated threat information, and have become an essential part of IPS operation. In fact, the signatures one finds in a typical IPS will originate primarily from threat research by experts.

The typical service involves multiple sources of threat information that are ingested to an aggregate database. Customers then hook up their systems to this threat feed as the basis for their intrusion detection and prevention activity. Human experts can also usually make excellent practical use of information from vendor threat feeds.

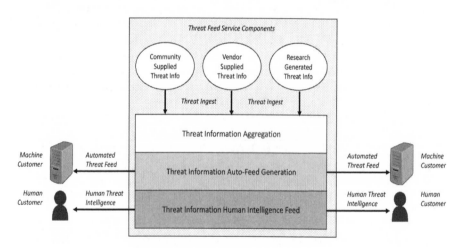

Figure 19-1. Typical Threat Feed Service

As one would expect, automated threat information feeds require the use of a well-defined structure for the descriptions of cyber attacks. Sharing unstructured descriptions based on text and diagrams might be useful for human experts, but to automate this function between machines requires well-defined syntactic and semantic structure.

The US Federal Government has created two standards called *Structured Threat Information Expression (STIX)* and *Trusted Automated Exchange of Indicator Information (TAXII)* that define the format, meaning, and protocol for real-time threat sharing. These standards are useful because they broaden the applicability of any compliant sharing.

In addition to structure, the requirements for high quality threat feeds include the following:

Timeliness – The ability for a security team to take meaningful action based on obtained threat information decreases with time. Thus, ensuring that threat information is shared quickly whenever possible is an important practical goal.

Context – Understanding the context of a shared threat is important to meaningful action. Sometimes this is obvious, as in the case where threat information is specific to a software package. Other times is might not be so obvious.

Trustworthiness – The degree to which shared threat information can be trusted is a critical concern. As with any form of intelligence, the source of the information is often just as important as the information itself.

The concept of trustworthiness of shared threat information leads naturally to the development of so-called *trust groups*. Often involving security operations center (SOC) staff in companies and government agencies, trust groups support the free flow of information without fear of unintended consequences. Sharing can be done without fear of leaks.

The classic counter-example involves a company sharing details of a hacking incident. This might sound innocent, but customers or investors might use the shared information to launch public criticism or legal action against the company. This simple risk prevents many organizations from sharing. It is the number one reason threat sharing has been such a challenge to date.

Many governments, including the United States, have nevertheless encouraged industry to arrange into sector-based trust groups. Some industries such as financial services have tended to do this well. Other sectors, such as telecommunications, have been less successful, perhaps because security is a marketing differentiator.

The typical arrangement for trust groups involves individuals within an enterprise establishing the first level of sharing. This might be overkill in smaller companies, but in larger firms with diverse business units, such sharing of threat information is non-trivial. So, this first level of internal information sharing often requires some effort to establish.

The second level of sharing comes within a sector, where different enterprise trust groups agree to share relevant data. Usually, this type of sharing is restricted to issues that are considered relevant to the unique vulnerabilities in that sector. For example, retail sector trust groups would share information related to credit card processing security.

A final level of sharing comes from different sectors sharing information across domains. This is the most powerful trust group concept, because it introduces diversity by enabling one sector to learn from the experiences of another. The software sector, for example, might gain useful insights from the telecommunications sector – and vice versa.

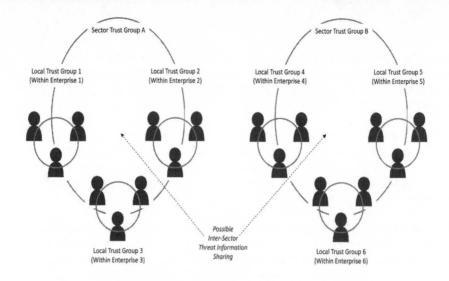

Figure 19-2. Trust Group Concept

Despite the familiar nature of humans sharing information, most threat feeds are, in fact, automated. A great example of a threat feed in common use involves the web security gateway that exists in most companies. As you might know, corporate environments typically police the types of websites allowed for use by employees, both for security and acceptable-use purposes.

To maintain an accurate list of website URLs that are recommended for blocking, security teams subscribe to threat feeds for web gateways, albeit with the recognition that blocking inappropriate sites might have less to do with security, and more with appropriateness. Nevertheless, the feed is real-time and automated between machines, often with no human inspection in the loop (see below).

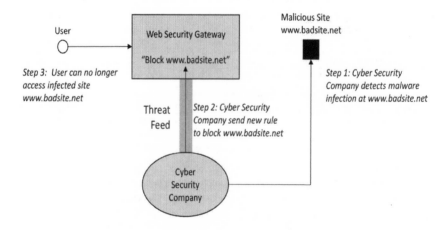

Figure 19-3. Website URL Threat Feed Architecture

Perhaps because threat information sharing is such an obviously useful method, many senior leaders, especially in government, tend to assign more weight to this safeguard than might be warranted. Because senior officials can easily conceptualize sharing, the solution tends to be prominently displayed in every speech, proposal, and guideline offered on cyber security.

Such emphasis provides an important lesson for anyone trying to make sense of cyber security. That is, just because a concept if easy-to-follow doesn't mean that its relative importance should be inflated. Behavioral analytics, cloud mediation, and scalable cryptography might be tough to understand, but that does not mean that they are any less important.

To summarize: For cyber security defenses such as IDS and DLP to work properly, threat information feeds are required to maintain real-time visibility into on-going threats. Both automated feeds and human sharing are enabled by participation in trust groups, which have the effect of reducing the concerns that someone in the sharing group will expose sensitive information about a hack.

In the next chapter, we put together some of the concepts we've learned so far into a familiar construct known as a *perimeter defense*. Usually designed as a control around an enterprise the perimeter has been the workhorse of enterprise cyber security for the past two decades. Despite weaknesses, the perimeter remains the most important safeguard in the modern enterprise.

20. Perimeter Defenses

The most important thing in terms of your circle of competence is not how large the area of it is, but how well you've defined the perimeter.

Warren Buffet

The functional controls we've examined – anti-malware, firewalls, intrusion prevention systems, and data leakage prevention systems – are typically arranged into a "protective wall" for an enterprise. This wall is called a *perimeter*, and it is positioned where a company connects to the Internet, or the enterprise network of a customer, partner, or supplier.

The perimeter is intended to separate an enterprise from external threats. It has been a primary control in the enterprise for many years. Perimeter effectiveness implies, of course, that internal users and resources can be trusted. We will see shortly that this broad assumption has significant drawbacks, including the reality that compromised or disgruntled insiders exist in most companies.

The specific controls that comprise a perimeter will vary from one enterprise to another, but almost all include the following capabilities:

Firewall – Often viewed as the primary component of a perimeter, the enterprise firewall implements the policies selected by the IT team, management, and security staff. It will include rules to protect requests coming both inbound to, and outbound from, the enterprise.

IPS – The IPS capability of a perimeter is designed to detect indicators of potential attack in real time so that rapid incident response can be quickly initiated. IPS devices usually collect packets either before or after the firewall is used to make decisions.

Anti-Malware – The scrubbing of traffic for the presence of malware, especially email payloads, is an important component of most perimeter designs. This is sometimes done by collecting the payload and analyzing it offline on a separate server.

Logging – Audit logs are usually included on a perimeter to keep track of security-relevant events including alarms from security devices. These logs are passed along to special enterprise security system called a *security information and event management (SIEM)* system that provides security teams with a comprehensive dashboard view of security-related activity.

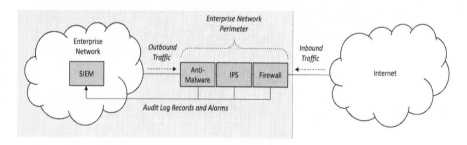

Figure 20-1. Simple Enterprise Perimeter

One advantage of a perimeter is that it delineates the internal and external nature of an enterprise network. For example, one can denote resources like physical servers as being "inside the perimeter," a designation that is usually called *private*. The problem is that most enterprise networks are complex, and keeping resources truly private is not easy.

In cases where an enterprise has multiple external connections, cyber security teams might be obliged to create multiple perimeters. Furthermore, because the inbound and outbound services across separate external connections will be different, these multiple perimeters will often include different security rules and devices.

The collective set of rules implemented across the perimeters of an enterprise is referred to as a *perimeter security policy*. As you might expect, managing and coordinating a complex perimeter security policy can be a challenge. For example, if one perimeter disallows outbound Web surfing, but another permits this, then employees can hunt around for the most permissive perimeter.

Ultimately, it is the obligation of the enterprise cyber security team to keep track of different perimeters, and to orchestrate coherent consistency between the respective rule sets. This task is accomplished via a combination of manual processes and automated tools including a common SIEM in the enterprise to keep track of all traffic. Figure 20-2 depicts how multiple perimeters can be arranged with a common SIEM into a more complex enterprise security architecture.

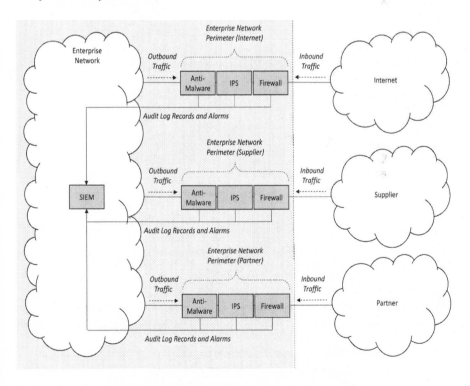

Figure 20-2. Multiple Perimeters in an Enterprise

The reality of modern enterprise perimeter design is that so many different inbound and outbound capabilities and services are required by companies, that the entire concept of perimeter protection is being seriously questioned. Example capabilities and services include mobile devices, tablets, cloud services, cloud email, remote access, and on and on.

The result is that most enterprise perimeters have become so porous that they barely differentiate private internal resources from public external ones. Furthermore, the potential exists, especially for larger organizations, that untrusted human beings might work inside the perimeter, and should not be trusted. This also calls into question the idea of internal versus external trust.

If we represent all gateways for an enterprise by a common perimeter circle with resources as boxes and service requests as arrows, then we can visually depict the clear differences between a simple perimeter with one gateway for external traffic versus a complex perimeter with multiple external gateways.

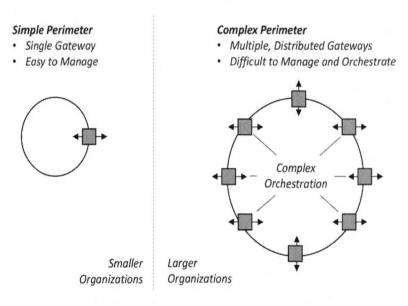

Figure 20-3. Simple Versus Complex Perimeter

In practice, most security experts refer to the totality of gateways into and out of an enterprise, regardless of whether the arrangement is simple or complex, as the enterprise perimeter. We will come back in later chapters to whether this is an optimal set-up to stop advanced attacks. It is true that to date, however, that virtually 100% of companies and agencies use a perimeter to stop external attacks.

To summarize: The enterprise perimeter includes functional controls such as firewalls, IP, DLP, and anti-malware, all connected to a SIEM. Complex enterprise requirements make it hard to maintain valid perimeters that maintain privacy, but the perimeter remains a workhorse in most enterprise networks.

Spotlight: Howard Schmidt

"Governments are starting to say, 'In order to best protect my country, I need to find vulnerabilities in other countries.' The problem is that we all fundamentally become less secure."

During Barack Obama's Presidential Administration, the decision was made correctly that a cyber security coordinator would be needed. Soon dubbed by the press as the role of Cyber Czar, the position would carry the responsibility of guiding and helping to manage the nation's cyber security objectives.

Unlike many senior appointments, where many potential candidates can fill a give role, relatively little debate was required in this case to determine who would be the best person to fill this important new cyber security position. Everyone agreed it must be Howard Schmidt.

With a career that began in the Air Force, including three tours of duty in Vietnam, Howard's life work included dedicated service to the Arizona Air National Guard and the Chandler Police Department in Arizona. This focus on law enforcement led Howard to the FBI, where he was soon working high tech cases in the Air Force Office of Special Investigations. This was Howard's introduction to computer security and before long he was directly involved in this burgeoning field.

After 9/11, President Bush asked him to serve as vice chair of the Critical Infrastructure Protection Board, and after a brief period serving in industry in the senior cyber security roles at eBay and Microsoft, he became the nation's first cyber security coordinator for President Obama. During his tenure, he created the US National Strategy for Trusted Identities in Cyberspace, which remains a landmark work.

After leaving government, Howard served in many different capacities as an entrepreneur, board member, and teacher. He left a wonderful legacy of contributions to cyber security from many different perspectives in government, industry, and academia.

21. Advanced Persistent Threats

Technological progress is like an axe in the hands of a pathological criminal.
Albert Einstein

One consequence of a complex perimeter is how it affords hackers the opportunity to gain access to the enterprise through one gateway, and to then make a clean getaway with stolen data out another. This process should not be surprising, since anyone who has ever locked up a home, school, or office knows that if you leave windows and doors open, then criminals will take advantage.

This process of traversing the enterprise to rummage around for useful data is known as an *advanced persistent threat* or *APT*. The entering and exiting through gateways is known as a *perimeter compromise* and the rummaging around is known as a *lateral traversal*. When you put these steps together, as shown in Figure 21-2, the result can be quite lethal for any company trying to protect its data.

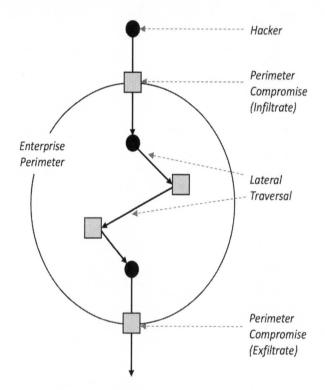

Figure 21-1. Components of an APT

The implementation steps of an APT are also straightforward: First, a technique known as *phishing* is almost always used in the first infiltrating, perimeter compromise step of an APT. Phishing involves crafting an email that entices a victim to click on a web link. Located behind that link will invariably be some malicious server that initiates a malware download to the unsuspecting user.

The malware will then load a *remote access tool* or *RAT* to the clicking user's computer. It's not unlike your company's IT administrator setting you up for remote access from home – except the RAT works in reverse. That is, the hacker sets up the victim's computer as the target of the remote access for the bad guys. It's a devious approach, and it's invisible to the user.

To make matters worse, if a malicious actor takes the time to perform background research on potentially unsuspecting victims, the phish works much better. For example, anyone who posts their interests on Facebook offers guidance on the type of content that might entice them to click. When such research is done in advance, we refer to the technique as *spear phishing*.

Figure 21-2 explicitly depicts the four steps of spear phishing attack, showing how they serve as the basis for an APT and how they correspond to weaknesses in the enterprise security architecture:

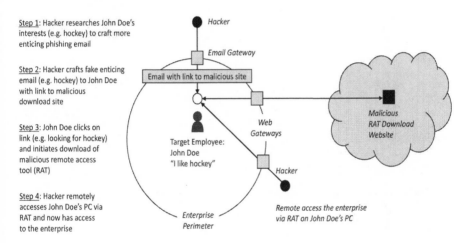

Figure 21-2. Spear Phishing as First Step of an APT

Once remote access has been established by hackers into the enterprise, the process commences of searching around for useful information to steal. You will recall that scanners are excellent ways to collect inventory, so it is not unusual for a hacker to launch a scanning activity from one hacked PC to find other PCs, servers, and resources worth exploring.

Another useful target during the lateral traversal phase involves exploration of the enterprise directory services, usually implemented with Microsoft's Active Directory. Virtually every enterprise in the world uses Active Directory to organize their computing resources. It thus provides APT hackers with a treasure trove of information about the enterprise.

The goal of the hacker in most APTs involves searching for information that has financial or strategic value. This can include databases of credit cards, files containing sensitive intellectual property (e.g. rocket designs from NASA), or personal health records of employees. The idea is to grab as much good stuff as possible while remote access is in place.

The middle letter in APT reminds us that attacks can be persistent. That is, hackers have been known to spend months or even years inside an enterprise shuffling around looking for useful data. This points to the weak security monitoring that exist in most organizations. Security teams are often embarrassed to admit that an APT has been hidden in their network for some time.

The final step in an APT involves the exfiltration of data from the enterprise. This is easy to do on any network that allows employees to visit external websites with no policy restrictions. In such cases, the hacker merely creates payload files on a hacked PC, and then freely visits malicious external drop sites to store the stolen goods.

Figure 21-3 illustrates the four steps of this latter portion of the APT attack, demonstrating how corresponding enterprise architectural weaknesses are exploited in the process:

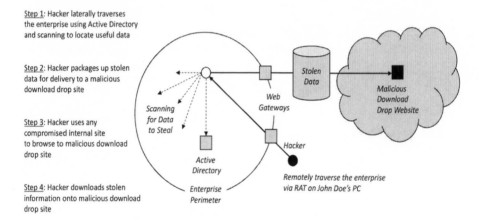

Figure 21-3. Completing an APT via Exfiltration

The simplicity of an APT might surprise you given the accepted notion that nation state actors can launch truly advanced attacks. One should remember, however, that even the best hackers will take the easy way into an enterprise if it is available. No good reason exists, for example, to dive through a partially open window if the front door is unlocked.

To summarize: advanced persistent attacks involve entry and exit through enterprise gateways. APTs are designed to traverse networks to locate useful data that can be stolen and exfiltrated. Nation state actors are most commonly behind APTs, often using spear phishing as the first point of entry. Poor monitoring enables continued risk of APT in the enterprise.

In the next chapter, we focus on the one area of cyber attacks that has the potential to change the nature of cyber threat – namely, *destructive attacks*. Unlike the theft of information, that is unacceptable, but that might not be sufficiently damaging to cause real business impact to an organization, destructive attacks might bring a target to its knees.

22. Destructive Attacks

Order without liberty and liberty without order are equally destructive.
Theodore Roosevelt

The cyber security community has obsessed on disclosure and denial of service these past two decades. That is, the primary focus of most major cyber attacks on individuals, business, and infrastructure has been leakage of information or blocking of access to services. These are the headlines we read every day in the cyber security press.

More recently, however, new forms of cyber-attack have begun to emerge that corrupt or degrade a computing resource. Ransomware is a good example; that is, malicious actors break into a system and then encrypt all the data. They then demand a ransom, usually in the form of untraceable Bitcoin, after which they provide the required key information to retrieve files.

This type of attack has the advantage of allowing users to recover, albeit only after paying a fee for such reconstitution. A more lethal form of corruptive attack has surfaced recently, that are truly *destructive* in nature. Designed to create the maximum disruption to a target, destructive cyber attacks can cause the operations to cease in a targeted company.

In 2012, for example, an oil company in the Middle East was the target of a serious destructive attack on their computers, resulting in a massive loss of their computing infrastructure. The targeted systems were corrupted by malicious software that affected the ability of the underlying system code to boot properly, resulting in a massive loss of hardware.

The most frightening aspect of destructive malware is that the associated attack patterns tend to mimic those found for advanced persistent threats. We know that APTs are difficult, if not impossible to stop, but the situation has been tolerable because data theft does not impede business operations. Destructive malware attacks can and will affect operations. Figure 22-1 contrasts the exfiltration and destruction goals of an APT.

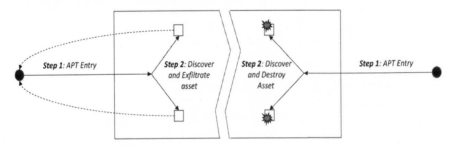

Figure 22-1. Comparing Disclosure and Destructive Attacks

A key insight regarding the lethality of destructive attacks is this: It is easier to *destroy* something, than it is to protect it. Furthermore, it is considerably simpler to dismantle or even delete something than it is to create that same object. For malicious actors who are intent on destroying, the associated process turns out to be relatively easy.

Two types of destructive attacks exist. The first type is recoverable, such as with ransomware attackers. In this case, the destruction might be temporary so long as some condition is met before restoration can proceed. As suggested earlier, this restoration for malware attacks usually involves the victim paying the attacker some amount of Bitcoin.

The second type of destructive attacks is permanent and non-recoverable. This case is obviously more serious. A typical permanent attack targets system level utilities such as low-level firmware that controls important functions such as the basic input and output of a computer. When this firmware, called BIOS, is attacked, the result is that the computer itself becomes largely unusable.

The solutions to destructive malware attacks range in scale and intensity. Sometimes, solutions can be conceptually simple. For example, BIOS attacks can be mitigated by preventing changes to the BIOS software. It is also true that virtually any cyber security solution that reduces APT and malware risk will also reduce destructive malware risk.

More typically, however, destructive malware is best mitigated through more complex means. In business, this implies increasing the resiliency of stored data and assets. More specifically, the strategy would be to make it harder for a malicious actor to create destruction problems because the targeted assets are easily restored. Well-designed back-up mechanisms are the most obvious example.

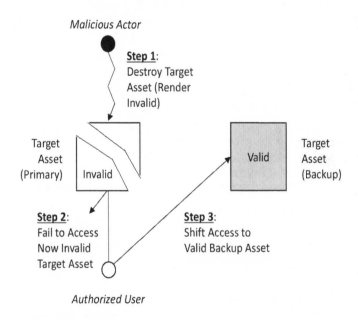

Figure 22-2. Reducing Destructive Malware Risk Through Back-Ups

The biggest concern cyber security experts have with the threat of destructive attack is the consequential impact such malicious efforts might have on essential services. Below are some example *potential* scenarios where an intense campaign of destructive attacks could have serious consequences on national critical infrastructure:

Banking and Finance – Destructive attacks could potentially target the ability of banks to maintain accurate information about customer accounts, and this could be the balance of your checking account.

Telecommunications – Destructive attacks on network infrastructure could impede the ability of local and global provides to maintain reliable mobile and landline services for customers.

Emergency Services – Destructive attacks to emergency response infrastructure could degrade the ability of first responders to deal with a life-critical situation.

Transportation – Destructive attacks could potentially target the ability of airlines, railroad, and traffic management systems to maintain safe, reliable transportation for citizens.

Power Grid – Destructive attacks on the power grid of any town, city, state, or region could have severe consequences on the entire area including potential serious loss of life.

Nuclear Power – Destructive attacks to any nuclear power plant are so considerable that the potential consequences should be obvious for any region where such a plant is located.

These example scenarios, thankfully, remain *potential* rather than actual. Small scale, contained glimpses of these scenarios certainly *have* occurred, but the consequences are so severe that every cyber security expert agrees that immediate action is required amongst infrastructure providers to ensure that no society should have to endure the effects of a serious destructive cyber attack.

To summarize: Where most cyber security emphasis to date has been on disclosure and denial of service threats, the potential for destructive malware introduces many lethal scenarios. While ransomware has been the most familiar example, the most consequential type of destructive attack would involve permanent damage to critical infrastructure.

In the next chapter, we will explore one approach to reducing the risk of APT, destructive malware, and other attacks. It involves establishing *compliance* with sets of common sense procedures and rules for how systems are administered and used. The compliance process has the advantage of being preventive, but the disadvantage of not being sufficient to stop significant attacks.

23. Security Compliance

Know the rules well, so that you can break them effectively.

Dalai Lama XIV

One approach to reducing cyber security risk involves *security compliance*. The theory is that by demanding that the enterprise comply with well-defined security rules, policies, procedures, and practices, the likelihood of a successful attack is reduced. Managers and government officials like this approach, because it involves the type of oversight activity they understand.

The compliance requirements in a corporate security policy are designed to help employees make good security decisions. They are intended to guide the decisions people make about administering systems, installing software, handling equipment, and so on. They try to bring discipline to the choices employees make that can influence security.

To do this, security policy requirements are usually embedded in business practices. For instance, the IT team might create practices to ensure that every employee PC is provisioned with proper anti-malware tools, or that every server in the company is scanned periodically for vulnerabilities. Compliance is about guiding good security decisions in an enterprise.

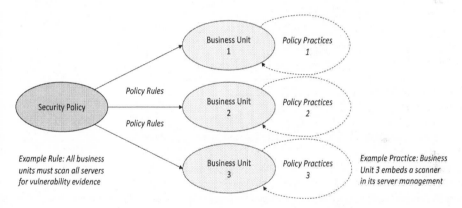

Figure 23-1. Implementing Policy Rules as Business Policy Practices

To see how security compliance programs can reduce enterprise cyber risk, let's examine how a sample set of requirements can potentially reduce the likelihood of an APT causing negative consequences. Let's suppose, for our example, that some organization decides to include the following five requirements in their compliance program:

Email Filtering – All inbound email content attachments must be scrubbed by anti-malware tools.

Employee Awareness – All employees must be periodically trained via awareness programs to not click on bad URLs.

Enterprise Scanning – Security teams must scan the enterprise periodically to ensure that sensitive data is not available for theft.

PC Security – All desktop PCs and laptops must have proper anti-malware tools installed and running always.

URL Filtering – Any outbound Web surfing can only be done to URLs that are known and categorized by the security team in advance.

If we superimpose these five example security compliance controls onto an APT attack diagram, we can see that they collectively reduce security risk in a substantive manner. That is, each requirement targets one component step in typical APT attack path, thus reducing the likelihood that a malicious actor will succeed in exfiltrating data (see below).

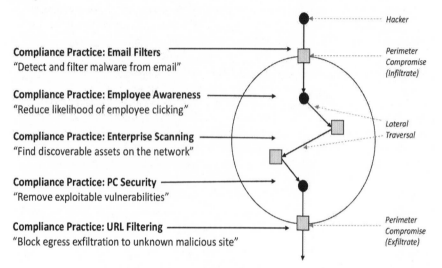

Figure 23-2. Reducing APT Risk Through Compliance

Security compliance programs are especially useful for reducing security risk when they are designed based on *general frameworks* that help guide the contents of a security policy. Many frameworks have been written by experts, and are made available to organizations through government agencies, standards groups, and other groups with authority.

The National Institute of Standards and Technology or NIST, for example, offers a security compliance framework called the *Framework for Improving Critical Infrastructure Cybersecurity* that can be used by medium and larger-sized companies to guide policy decisions. The framework also guides how compliance decisions can be embedded in organizational business practices.

The process of writing policies, designing associated practices, and demonstrating compliance with framework requirements is referred to in business as *governance, risk, and compliance* or GRC. While virtually every cyber security team will attest to the essential nature of GRC in reducing risk, most experts are also quick to point out the significant problems associated with compliance tasks.

The first problem is that too many different compliance frameworks tend to be levied on businesses. One framework, for example, might demand six character passwords, whereas another might demand eight character passwords, and still another might demand strong passwords. This creates considerable paperwork, meetings, reports, and other work for security teams.

A second problem is that compliance can drive a security team in directions that have nothing to do with cyber security. For example, if a set of policy rules dictates good PC security, then the associated compliance program often involves effort trying to locate the enterprise PCs. This inventory process is important, but it wastes security expert resources on non-security tasks.

A third problem is that compliance programs are often levied as punishment after an attack. Government organizations, for example, like to follow up a corporate cyber attack with severe requirements for additional compliance – as if this is the only means for reducing risk. The reality is that most new compliance requirements are redundant with existing controls, and hence have little incremental impact.

To summarize: Compliance programs based on frameworks are excellent means for reducing cyber risk in an enterprise. They involve policies and rules that guide good security decisions by the people in an organization. The problem is that too much weight is given to compliance in risk reduction, not to mention that multiple frameworks can sometimes be counter-productive to security teams.

The next chapter introduces an advanced risk reduction technique that is popular with security experts. It involves the use of *security analytic* methods to pore through collected data in search of indicators of attack. Such analytics are promising, because they combine human skill with expert algorithms to optimize the use of audit log information from the network.

24. Security Analytics

The most valuable commodity I know of is information.

Gordon Gekko
(From the movie "Wall Street")

To prevent cyber attacks from wreaking havoc on a network, many security teams have turned to a new form of protection known as *security analytics*. This method of protection involves gathering security-related information into stored repositories, and then running algorithms on the data to detect anomalies. Human assistance is generally required to guide the process toward accurate response conclusions.

We alluded earlier to a tool known as a *security information and event management (SIEM)*, which collects log records, activity trace information, and alarms into a large security database. From this database, tools perform basic comparison and correlation operations to determine if attacks might be brewing. These operations are called *security analytics*.

The two main methods of security analytics involve either pattern matching of data to known security signatures or profile-based examination of data against a known behavioral profile. In both cases, security teams must have a general understanding of what constitutes a security attack, and the security analytics tasks are used to detect evidence of such risk.

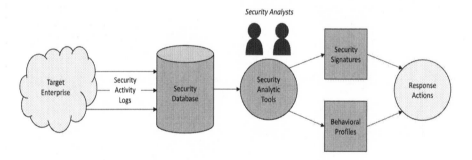

Figure 24-1. Two Methods of Security Analytics

Our discussion in a previous chapter on anti-malware methods offered an overview of how signatures are used to describe attacks, and how these are used to pattern-match against collected activity logs. As we discussed, signatures tend to be fixed descriptions of attack methods, and can be easily bypassed through variants. This aspect of security analytics need not be repeated further here.

Instead, we will focus here on the behavioral profiling method, which has been shown in recent years to be relatively successful in detecting cyber attack conditions. The way behavioral profiling works in the typical enterprise case involves four discrete security analytic steps, which operate dynamically, continuously, and in parallel:

Baselining – This task creates a baseline profile description of behaviors that are considered normal.

Observing – This task collects information about the behaviors that are occurring.

Correlating – This task compares and assesses the degree of conformance for observed behaviors with respect to baselined profiles.

Learning – This task feeds knowledge of whether previous correlative conclusions resulted in useful response actions.

These four tasks collectively make up the security analytics ecosystem in most enterprise networks. Normal behavior is profiled, actual behavior is observed, correlation between the two is used to generate response, and then learning activities try to improve the overall process (see below).

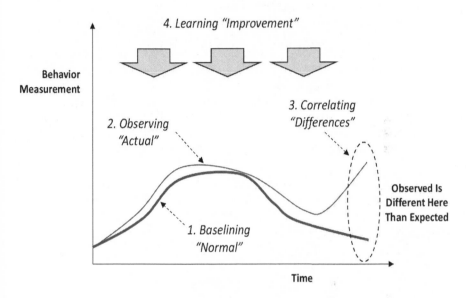

Figure 24-2. Security Analytics Task Ecosystem

A simple example of correlative analysis from security data can be seen by looking at three different software applications that might be running in an enterprise. Suppose that a human resources application, an invoice processing application, and a sales support application are all hosted in an enterprise and exhibit a degree of normal behavior during the week.

Specifically, let's assume that the three applications build up in the morning, peak around mid-afternoon, and then wane as the day progresses. All three applications, we can assume, are quiet in the evening and on weekends. A graph of their behavior using histogram counts of computing resource use might look as follows:

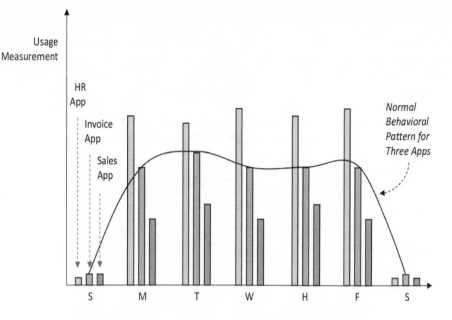

Figure 24-3. Histogram of Normal Application Behavior

Let's suppose that during an expected quiet period, such as a weekend, all three applications begin to display unusually busy usage. This would display in the context of collected data as an anomaly between expected and observed behavior. Simple security analytics would identify this correlative issue and would initiate response activity.

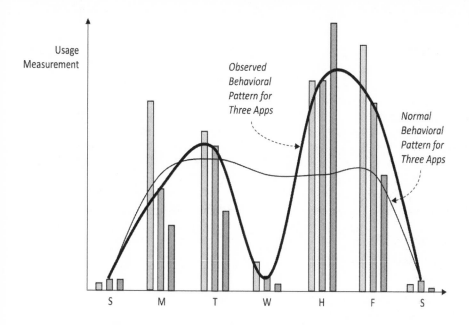

Figure 24-4. Histogram of Observed versus Profiled Behavior

Obviously, in a practical setting, the security analytic task would be much more complex, and would demand more subtle interpretation of the data. If, for example, thousands of applications were operating in an environment with less obvious busy and quiet periods, then identifying anomalies might require more careful data analysis. This usually dictates the use of advanced technologies to support analytics.

The idea here is that a technique known as *management by exception* introduces the possibility that observed differences from the norm might signal that an attack is underway. This is a powerful security analytics concept because it uncovers possible attack indicators without the need to include predictive signatures in advance.

Security analytics as a discipline is in its infancy. Every day, professional analysts, now known by many as cyber hunters, invent new ways to analyze data to uncover early indicators. They are also using security analytics to improve the automated tools that exist in their enterprise, including SIEM collection and processing.

To summarize: Techniques for security analytics have emerged that complement signature processing via profile-based analysis of observed behaviors. Such analysis focuses on detecting deviations from the norm as a management by exception means for uncovering the possibility that cyber attack indicators might be present in the data.

In the next chapter, we focus on a specific type of attack known as *distributed denial of service*, that requires an especially sharp real-time capability for analysis. The irony is that despite the obvious wave-like effects that are experienced after a DDOS attack, only subtle indicators are generally present for analysts in advance of such attacks.

25. Distributed Denial of Service

An overflow of good converts to bad.

William Shakespeare

When an enterprise hooks up to the Internet, the amount of data that can flow across that connection is dictated by the size of the circuit purchased from the Internet service provider (ISP). A typical large business, for example, might reach the Internet across an ISP connection that can handle ten billion bits of data every second (10 gigabits per second or 10 Gbps), which is an enormous volume.

Nevertheless, the possibility exists that hackers can find a way to exceed the connection capacity using a botnet or other means. So, for example, if a business can accept 5 Gbps inbound from the Internet, then a successful *denial of service* attack would involve greater than 5 Gbps inbound, thus overwhelming the connection and isolating the enterprise from any other inbound traffic.

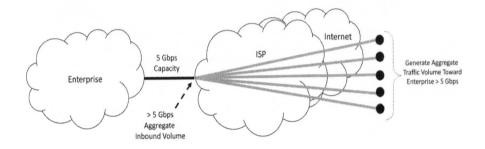

Figure 25-1. Inbound Denial of Service Attack

When a denial of service attack involves a botnet with many distributed endpoint sources, we refer to the attack as a *distributed denial of service* or *DDOS*. The two fundamental concepts involved in a DDOS attack are *reflection* and *amplification*. Reflection involves Alice asking Bob a question, and having the response go to some other source. Amplification involves a small question producing a large response.

Combining reflection and amplification can be illustrated by imagining a speaker in front of a large audience barking a low sound to everyone present, but to have that bark then amplified into a large sound that is redirected from everyone toward a target – perhaps someone seated in the front row. The effect of this would be like everyone in the audience shouting at the target individual.

From a TCP/IP perspective, DDOS attacks are accomplished via botnets issuing a series of requests toward some service that amplifies its response. The Domain Name System (DNS) is an example of such a service. These requests are made from the spoofed source IP address of the target. When the amplified responses to these requests are made, they are directed in aggregate toward the target.

If each bot makes requests to a variety of DNS servers for information, but spoofs its source IP address as 1.2.3.4, which is the address of the target victim, then the amplified

DNS responses would be sent from the DNS servers to 1.2.3.4. The result is that potentially huge volumes of DNS information would barrage the victim's 1.2.3.4 gateway, thus removing its ability to service other inbound traffic.

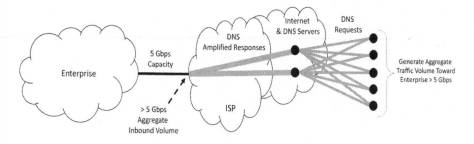

Figure 25-2. DNS Reflection and Amplification in Botnet-Originated DDOS

Doing the math on botnet-originated DDOS attacks produces some frightening conclusions from the perspective of national critical infrastructure protection. If a bot running on a home PC, for example, can originate one million bits per second or 1 Mbps, then you can do the math on how big an aggregate DDOS attack might be for botnets of different sizes.

In addition, by comparing botnet-originated DDOS size with the capacity of inbound gateway connections for enterprise networks, you can estimate the amount of damage that can be created by different botnets. This exercise suggests that an inflection point occurs at ten thousand-member botnets at 1 Mbps attack capacity, which can fill up a common 10 Gbps enterprise gateway.

Number of Bots	Traffic from Each Bot	Amount of DDOS Traffic Generated	
1,000	1,000,000 bps (1 Mbps)	1 Gbps	*Size of Small/Medium Enterprise Gateway*
10,000	1,000,000 bps (1 Mbps)	10 Gbps	*Size of Typical Large Enterprise Gateway*
100,000	1,000,000 bps (1 Mbps)	100 Gbps	*Size of Typical ISP Backbone*

Figure 25-3. Botnet DDOS Attack Size Calculations

The critical infrastructure implications here should be obvious. That is, for any essential network service that provides some service to society that cannot be replaced, or whose removal could lead to loss of safety or lives, the potential of a DDOS attack becomes unacceptable. Given the relatively modest work required to build a ten thousand-member botnet, it becomes easy to interrupt infrastructure.

Perhaps worse is the potential for botnets to be constructed with millions of member devices. Consider, for example, that with the new Internet of Things or IoT, billions of poorly secured devices have been scattered across the global Internet. If botnet begin to efficiently harness the attack capacity of these devices, then DDOS attacks of immense strength might be produced.

The solution generally used to reduce the risk of DDOS involves upstream filtering from ISPs or managed security solutions provider. This filtering involves real-time detection by the ISP of any activity that *appears* to be inbound DDOS being targeted to the enterprise. If this looks to be occurring, then the ISP quickly reroutes the inbound traffic to firewalls designed to filter the traffic.

If you're wondering how the firewalls determine good traffic from DDOS traffic, then you are asking the correct question. It is not easy; but DDOS firewalls, which are usually called *scrubbers*, use heuristics such as similar payloads from multiple sources, a common time in which the traffic was sent, similar packet characteristics of traffic being sent, and so on.

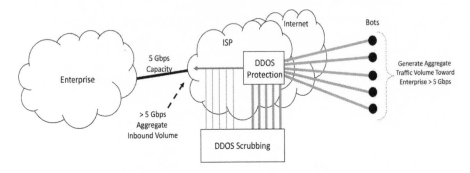

Figure 25-4. DDOS Scrubbing by Service Providers

The practical experience has been that this scrubbing technique works reasonably well, but that it requires constant vigilance, along with some operational luck. That is, if a significant series of concurrent DDOS attacks were to be initiated at the same time to the same set of targets, it's unclear whether service providers would have the ability to stop the associated volumes.

To summarize: DDOS attacks from botnets are relatively easy to construct and they can generate large traffic volumes toward a victim. The potential for DDOS attacks to disrupt critical services is immense. Service providers address the risk by diverting traffic to scrubbing complexes, but this solution does not scale to multiple simultaneous attacks. IoT complicates matter as well.

In the next chapter, we examine cyber security issues that originate on the *operating system*. This is a critical concern for *endpoint* PCs and mobiles both in the enterprise and on your home desktop. As you will see, operating system security can be a bit messy, with proper risk management often requiring day-to-day administrative attention.

26. Operating System Security

Unix is basically a simple operating system, but you have to be a genius to understand the simplicity.

Dennis Ritchie

The most basic concept in computer science is that underlying hardware, such as processors, memory, and input/output controllers, are managed by *operating system* software. This is true for every computer, including PCs, servers, mobile devices, gaming consoles, and even wind turbine controllers. Popular operating systems include Android, Windows, and Linux.

The functions of an operating system include processing of instructions and storage of information. These are carried out by software entities called *processes* and *objects*. A process executes on behalf of a user, whereas an object is a passive information repository such as a file or directory. As you would expect, operating system security involves policy enforcement amongst processes and objects.

Separation is one such policy, and it ensures non-interference of processes and objects. For example, if processes are executing on behalf of users Alice and Bob, then the operating system enforces separation controls to make sure that no information leaks from one process to another, and that no malicious effects might be felt by one from the other. This process separation can be depicted as shown in the figure below:

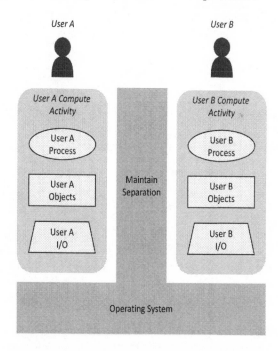

Figure 26-1. Process Separation in an Operating System

Policies are enforced on operating systems using software mechanisms, the most important of which is a called *access control*. An access control is used to implement rules such as keeping the objects of one process away from another. Access controls are also made available at the application level on systems that might want to separate different users or downloaded apps.

The first type of access control is called *discretionary access control* or *DAC*. This gives the owner of an object the ability to make policy decisions about its objects. The advantage is the flexibility afforded users, but a grave disadvantage is that if malware infects a given application or user, then the malware can take advantage of DAC to change settings on objects.

The second type of access control is called mandatory access control or MAC. This is controlled by system administrators or owners on behalf of users and applications. MAC is often put in place to help ensure that users cannot make bad decisions that could have a harmful effect on the entire system. They also help reduce the risk of application-level malware creating harmful effects.

In the early days of computer security, special policy rules were created for MAC on operating systems that would not permit application-level processes to modify system-level controls or read super sensitive stored information. These policies, pioneered by men such as Len LaPadula, David Bell, and Ken Biba, had a major influence on operating system security design in the 1980s and 1990s.

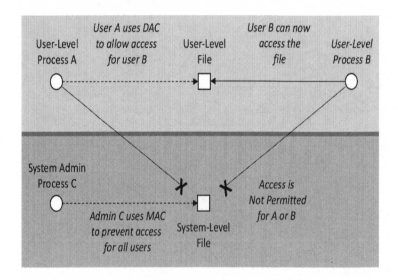

Figure 26-2. Protecting System Files with DAC and MAC

An additional security-relevant component of every operating system is the *audit log*. As we explained in an earlier chapter, this log chronicles the activity of processes on objects, and can be used for identifying indicators of possible cyber attack planning or execution.

Logs exist on operating systems at both the application and system level, each offering a unique vantage point on observed activity.

The biggest challenge of operating system security involves assurance that the software cannot be subverted by hackers to undermine applications. This challenge becomes obvious when one considers that applications are built on the foundations of an operating system. Hacks to this foundation thus undermine the security of anything it supports.

As a result, the security industry has developed a cottage industry maintaining and managing information about vulnerabilities to system-level software, with great emphasis on operating systems. Some cyber security companies even specialize in helping to identify and organize these vulnerabilities and their associated software fixes, usually called *patches.*

The patching process, it turns out, is an especially difficult activity, because it requires considerable coordination, update, test, and integration for it to work seamlessly. Apple is an example of a company that closely controls all aspects of the security patch process for its operating system. Google, in contrast, works with different groups including ISPs to issue patches. Both models have pros and cons.

All security patching for operating systems and any other software share certain properties. All originate with a bug introduced to the software during the development process. This is followed by detection of the bug, usually by users of the software. The resulting steps include patch development, patch testing, patch issuance, and then distributed patch deployment by users.

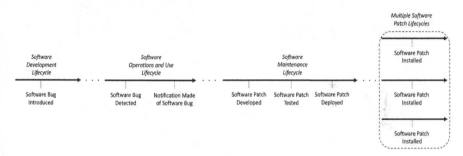

Figure 26-3. Security Patch Lifecycle Process

The degree to which an organization has patched its known security problems is a key indicator of security risk. A major problem emerges, however, when brand new security vulnerabilities become known, and this is common in modern operating systems. These zero-day vulnerabilities are perhaps the most difficult challenges in cyber security, particularly for critical infrastructure groups.

To summarize: Operating system security involves separation of processes and objects to enforce policy. Access control mechanisms in the form of DAC and MAC enforce these policies, and audit logs keep track of relevant activity. Patching is a particularly challenging issue for operating systems because of the degree of coordination required among different groups.

In the next chapter, we take a look at a concept that builds upon the idea of operating system security, virtual security. Virtualization is a promising and exciting area in all areas of computer science, especially with the heavy adoption of cloud environments by many organizations. As you will see, the agile and clever design of virtual security solutions allows for new possibilities that would otherwise be too dangerous on a conventional operating system.

27. Virtual Security

I accept reality and dare not question it.

Walt Whitman

It was accepted for many years that each computer would have one dedicated operating system to provide an interface between user applications and system hardware. In the early days of computing, it was discovered that by *time-sharing* the focus of this operating system quickly between users, the illusion could be created that each user owned the entire system. This was called *multi-tasking*.

More recently, however, computer system designers have identified a clever way to optimize hardware resources. Specifically, designers have used *virtualization* to create multiple operating systems running on the same underlying hardware. A resultant set of *virtual machines* emerges to create a view for users that they each have complete control of the hardware resources.

To manage the different virtual machines running on a given system, a special piece of software has been invented called a *hypervisor*. This management software resides between the underlying hardware and the virtual machines on that system. It is intended to coordinate and orchestrate the operating of virtual machines as they share underlying resources.

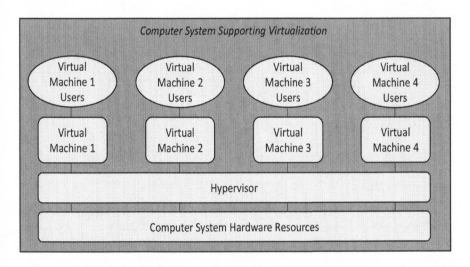

Figure 27-1. Hypervisor Control of Virtual Machines on a Computer

The security issues that arise in the context of hypervisor-supported virtualization should be obvious. First, the problem of a hacker penetrating one virtual machine to undermine the others must be resolved. The hypervisor is tasked with preventing this scenario by separating and segregating resource usage between the respective virtual machines.

Second, a security vulnerability in the underlying hardware could cascade to all supported virtual machines. This reduces the attack surface for malicious actors because a single targeted hardware exploit would cascade to multiple virtual operating systems. The hypervisor might help, but improved hardware protection from external attacks is more generally required.

The real security implication of virtualization, however, is its enablement of new technology known as *cloud service*. That is, virtual machines enable expansion of computing infrastructure in a way that was previously impossible, if only to reduce costs. Virtualization allows massive increases in the efficient use of computing hardware, and has thus changed how the world uses on-line services.

The corporate data center, for example, consisted for many years of hardware components, stacked on top of each other, and wired together for the purposes of supporting applications and services. This arrangement required expensive infrastructure, floor space, power, cooling, and physical security. It also required a great deal of time to put in place and then administer.

With virtualization, however, the data center has transformed to a series of virtual machine-hosted capabilities called workloads that are all executing on generic underlying hardware that is commonly and uniformly managed. The resultant infrastructure, when it is located inside a corporate enterprise, is referred to as a *private cloud*.

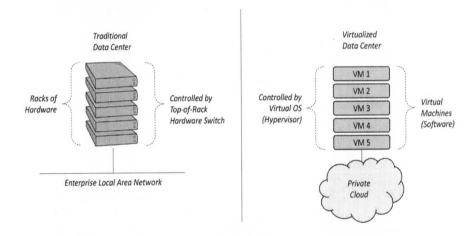

Figure 27-2. Virtualization Supporting Private Cloud-Based Data Centers

The security obligation for virtual, private cloud infrastructure involves a shift from racked hardware controlled by a special component known as a top-of-rack switch, to a software-based collection of virtual machines controlled by a cloud-based operating system. This shift results in significantly increased flexibility in an enterprise data center, as well as greatly reduced hardware costs.

The ability to dynamically create virtualized computing allows for many new advanced types of cyber security protections. A common example of such involves creating a special type of virtual container within which malware can be tested to determine if it is lethal. This process is often referred to as *sandbox testing*.

Sandbox testing involves first detecting malware that might be present, perhaps in a downloaded attachment to an email. This would be followed by the suspicious file or download being placed into a virtual computing environment that is separated from real assets and resources. It is then tested thoroughly in that environment to determine if there is truly malware present.

If malware is present, there is no way for it to damage real resources, because the whole test process is done on its own virtual machine, also sometimes referred to as a containerized environment. If no malware is present, then the tested attachment or payload would be allowed to proceed to the real target environment for normal handling (see below).

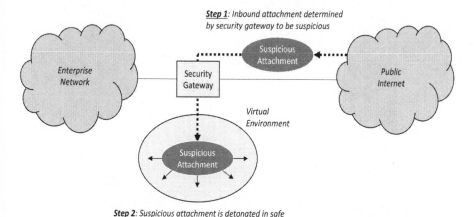

Figure 27-3. Sandbox Testing in Virtual Environments

The power of virtualization in providing advanced cyber security constructs is tough to over-estimate. The ability, for example, to dynamically create new expanded infrastructure in real time to absorb detected denial of service attacks creates a powerful new capability for increasing the resiliency of target enterprise to availability problems.

To summarize: The applications for virtualization in cyber security are boundless. As cloud services become more and more pervasive, the agile nature of dynamic virtual containers will cause virtual security solutions to continue growing in presence. Sophisticated solutions that use virtualization for malware detections and software detonation, such as with sandbox testing, are promising and powerful defensive options.

In the next chapter, we begin to address a truly modern security issue – namely, the protection of information and assets that are stored in a new type of computing and networking service known as the *cloud*. This is the most pervasive concept in information technology today, and it is entirely possible that the book you are reading right now is being made available to you in the cloud.

28. Cloud Security

Cloud computing is often far more secure than traditional computing, because companies like Google and Amazon can attract and retain cyber security personnel of a higher quality than many governmental agencies.

Vivek Kundra, Former CIO of the US

Most organizations have begun moving their applications to public cloud services such as Amazon Web Services or Microsoft Azure. A major advantage of this shift is improved application accessibility for employees, partners, customers, and suppliers. This involves clicking on apps from mobile devices, rather than having to navigate complex remote access procedures to the enterprise local area network.

The shift to cloud introduces several cyber security issues for users and organizations. For example, enterprise security teams need to understand how cloud service providers handle their data in the cloud. That is, when files are pushed to cloud, or when applications are hosted in cloud, it may not be clear how these assets are managed.

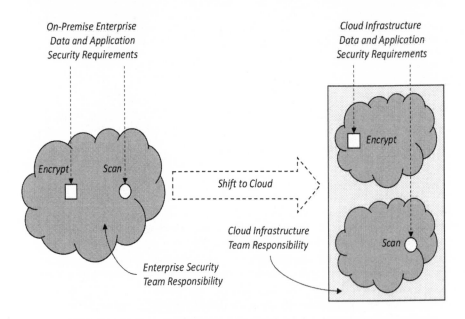

Figure 28-1. Security Requirements Shift from On-Premise to Cloud

In addition to data and resources shifting to cloud, the corresponding functional security controls are also migrating to cloud. As explained earlier, the most common solution in enterprise involves a firewall-based perimeter stretching around enterprise assets. As resources move to cloud, they naturally become resident outside the perimeter, and hence uncontrolled.

A useful solution involves smaller, more customized perimeters around cloud-resident resources. Computing experts refer to these cloud resources as *workloads*, and security engineers refer to these smaller perimeters wrapped around workloads as *micro-perimeters*. One might view micro-perimeters as shrink-wrapped workload security.

A major enabling technology for micro-perimeters involves something called *virtualization*, which involves using special software that creates new "virtual computers" on top of real, physical computers. This allows new security functions to be created using only software, which allows shrink-wrapped micro-perimeters to be built without the security team having to spend money on hardware.

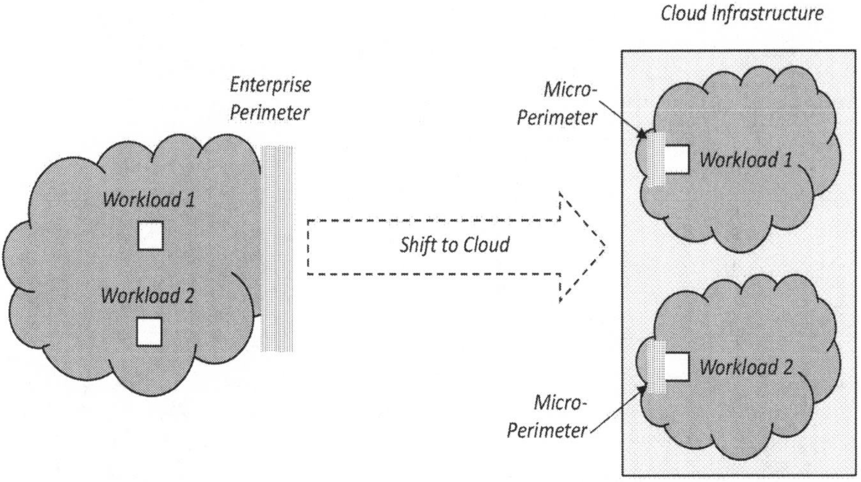

Figure 28-2. From Enterprise Perimeter to Cloud-Based Micro-Perimeters

In addition to micro-perimeters, many cloud security deployments include a specially designed component that resides on a network between users and cloud applications. This component is called a *cloud access security broker* or *CASB*, and it looks like a security filter resident in front of clouds. CASB functions are especially useful in enterprise designs that use multiple cloud services.

This use of multiple cloud services, combined with continued use of an existing, legacy perimeter enterprise results in a *hybrid cloud architecture*. Modern enterprise networks are evolving quickly to hybrid solutions, because they combine the best elements of highly accessible cloud services, with the practical need to maintain some legacy systems behind an existing perimeter.

CASB functions are also useful for enterprise networks that must include connections to specific IT functions like databases or human resource systems that are offered by their vendors in the cloud. They help to arbitrate access and maintain compliance in complex hybrid cloud networks that include legacy perimeter, multiple cloud workloads, and cloud-resident IT services.

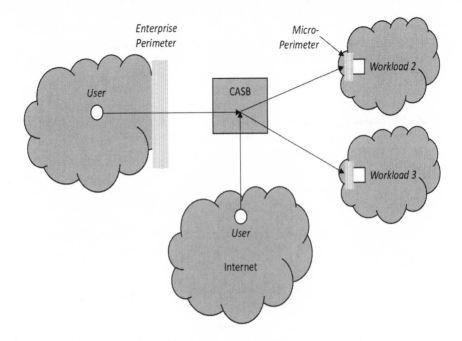

Figure 28-3. Hybrid Cloud Architecture with CASB

The shift to hybrid cloud is accelerating, not only because security solutions are increasingly available, but also because IT teams save quite a bit of money with cloud services. Furthermore, users with mobile devices like the convenience of gaining access to corporate resources in the cloud, versus having to connect through an official corporate network.

To summarize: Cloud security involves improving knowledge of how cloud service providers handle data. The functional controls for protecting cloud workloads include micro-segments that shrink wrap security controls around cloud-resident resources, and cloud access security brokers that reside between users and cloud assets, usually in a hybrid architecture.

The next chapter continues with our narrative on modern cyber security controls for evolving infrastructure. The focus on *mobility* in both enterprise and personal computing use has been one of the great shifts in modern society. As one might expect, hackers have noticed this shift, and the result is an increase in cyber security focus for mobile devices, applications, and infrastructure.

29. Mobile Security

*What we want to do is make a leapfrog product that is way smarter than any
mobile device has ever been, and super-easy to use. This is what iPhone is. OK?
So, we're going to reinvent the phone.*

Steve Jobs

If you are like most people in business today, then you are more dependent on your mobile
phone than on any other piece of equipment, including your PC. The mobile revolution has
caused every business and citizen to rethink how they interact with the world. Such
interaction has been obvious for teenagers dropping selfies onto Instagram, but it has now
become just as clear for everyone.

As you might expect, hackers have noticed this shift in emphasis to mobility, and
have adjusted their attack strategies accordingly. More and more cyber attacks to mobile
phones emerge every day, and security experts have now begun to establish technology to
address the growing threat. The specific security threats to mobility can be partitioned into
three categories:

Mobile Device Security – This involves the security protection of device access,
device operating systems, and device hardware. For businesses, this can include inventory
and management of mobile devices as well.

Mobile App Security – This involves determination as to the relative security of
mobile apps in public download stores. It stands to reason that security consideration
should influence whether to download a given mobile app.

Mobility Infrastructure Security – This involves the nuts and bolts of assuring that
hackers cannot cause security problems for mobile infrastructure operators. Mobile service
providers (MSPs) focus on this area.

The most obvious threat to mobile device security involves unauthorized access to
lost devices. Imagine leaving your iPhone on the seat in a taxi, and the sort of havoc this
might cause to your life or business if some untrustworthy person found your device. They
could access your email, social networks, work-related services, and other aspects of your
personal and business life.

The solution to this problem is improved authentication in the form of unlocking
PINs, passwords, and biometric thumbprints. These minor nuisances offer peace of mind
for users who might misplace their device. Certainly, there are risks that single factor PINs
on devices can be guessed (e.g., your PIN might be your zip code or portion of your cell
number), but security is still increased.

A more complex issue for mobile users involves operating system-level procedures
that can be used to change the underlying system. Jailbreaks, for example, can be
performed in tethered (i.e., connected to a computer) and untethered manner to affect the
boot sequence on a mobile device. Such clever methods are usually focused on freeing a
given device from MSP restrictions.

Considerable debate exists as to whether jailbreaks are acceptable. Most hackers
believe that once they buy a mobile device, they should be free to do as they wish with the
underlying operating system software – and one can certainly make the case that they are
correct. Different countries have different views on this and the legality of jailbreaking will
continue to evolve.

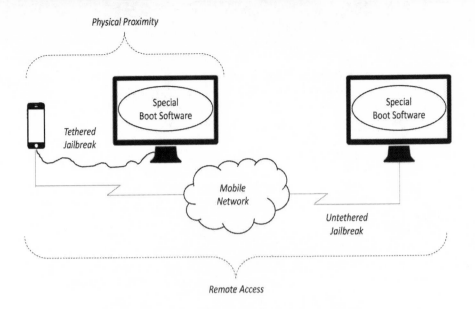

Figure 29-1. Tethered and Untethered Mobile Jailbreaks

The cyber security issues for mobile apps are more consistently agreed upon. No one, including the hacking community, believes it is acceptable for a mobile app to be advertised as doing one thing, but to actually do something different and more nefarious. This is the definition of Trojan horse, and with mobility, this usually implies the use of *spyware*.

The typical spyware scenario involves snooping software being embedded into a seemingly useful mobile app that will be willingly downloaded by unsuspecting users. Once installed, the spyware serves as a software collection point for data of interest. Location, contacts, email, and pictures are common targets. Most users barely notice that the spyware is even running.

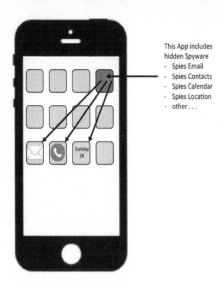

Figure 29-2. Typical Spyware App on Mobile

Mobile infrastructure security issues are more complex, ranging from legacy circuit switched weaknesses, to possible hacks targeting the availability of mobile services in certain focused regions. With the increased dependence of citizens and businesses on mobile services, cyber attacks to mobile infrastructure have potentially significant consequences.

One example attack on mobile infrastructure involves a distributed denial of service attack on some mobile entry point. This could be a WiFi hotspot, a mobile service provider cell tower, or other point of connectivity for wireless devices. The idea would be to overwhelm the connection point with service requests, presumably initiated by malware.

A simple version of this mobile infrastructure attack could occur in a downloadable Trojan horse mobile app that purports to do something useful, but that includes hidden functionality designed to overwhelm a carrier network. Perhaps it is an app that manages pictures, or changes the sound of your voice, or virtually anything that might cause people to download.

Once downloaded, if the app accepts remote commands, then mobile devices with this app might be commanded to create DDOS traffic. Perhaps the app is designed to detect WiFi signals in Starbucks shops, or LTE signals from a Tier 1 carrier, and at a designated time, to flood each targeted network. Location information from the mobiles could help control the accuracy of the attack.

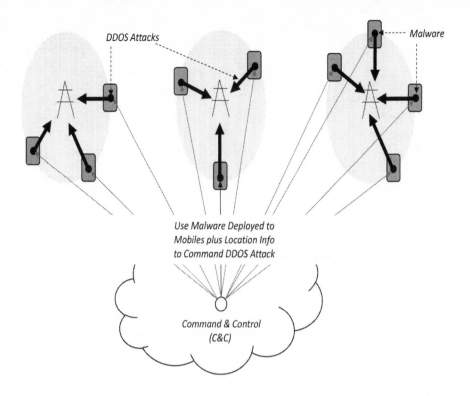

DDOS Attacks

Malware

Use Malware Deployed to
Mobiles plus Location Info
to Command DDOS Attack

Command & Control
(C&C)

Figure 29-3. Mobile App DDOS Attack

Mobile service providers offer solutions to this issue, including the ability to quickly filter the malware traffic to their tower. This is not easy and requires clever use of technology such as spread spectrum deployment, which is hard to jam. The optimal solution, however, stops the connection request on the device, even though this requires coordination with the device owner.

Suffice it to say that a mobile DDOS attack illustrates the type of issue that a mobile service provider must consider with respect to threat. As the degree of complexity and skill associated with mobile attacks increases, the corresponding required effort by the provider grows as well. We should all be glad that this is taken seriously, given the importance of mobile service to our lives.

To summarize: Mobile security issues require attention on the mobile device, mobile app ecosystem, and supporting mobility infrastructure from carriers. All have their respective challenges with respect to reducing cyber risk, but all are increasingly important as citizens and business continue to rely more on mobile services.

In the next chapter, we continue with the theme of *infrastructure security* and its impact on society. The greatest challenge for business and citizens regarding infrastructure security is the high level of dependence that exists for network, cloud, and application providers to ensure proper infrastructure protection. Governments also play a role, but this is complicated by international differences.

30. Infrastructure Security

No gluing together of partial studies of a complex nonlinear system can give a good idea of the behavior of the whole.

Murray Gell-Mann

For automation to be useful in society, underlying technical support is required. As an example, mobile phone services are essential to our personal and professional lives, but these services are only possible if mobile devices are manufactured, mobile networks are built and maintained, and support functions for billing, management, and security are kept working.

The collective term for this underlying support is *infrastructure*, and when the associated services are considered essential, we refer to the associated underlying support as *critical infrastructure*. An additional popular definition of critical infrastructure is any underlying service support that, if removed, would create serious problems for society.

Examples of critical infrastructure include the support systems for transportation, government, energy, telecommunications, and finance. As you might expect, if any of these infrastructure components became degraded or unavailable, the consequences to society would be severe. The power infrastructure in most countries offers the most obvious illustration of this potential trouble.

A problem with critical infrastructure security is that practitioners tend to apply protections that were designed for smaller systems. This is an issue, because the needs of a large and small computer system can be as different as one might find for, say, a jumbo jet and bicycle. Maintenance, monitoring, trust, and compliance are example factors that are directly influenced by size, scale, and scope.

Support Function	Large Systems (High Scale and Scope)	Small Systems (Low Scale and Scope)
Maintenance	Automated	Manual
Monitoring	Distributed	Centralized
Trust/Assurance	Interdependencies	Monolithic
Compliance	Non-Uniform	Uniform

Figure 30-1. Infrastructure Security for Large and Small Systems

Smaller systems require the types of cyber protections that are described in detail throughout this book. Authentication, access control, and encryption are examples of familiar controls used commonly. The demands of infrastructure, however, especially in support of critical services, introduce considerably more risk, primarily due to the increased consequences of attack.

As such, cyber security solutions have emerged that are essential for protecting critical infrastructure. They have evolved through years of practical experience operating infrastructure in the presence of increasingly severe cyber security offensive pressure. They have also evolved in a different direction than many of the small-scale controls you might be more familiar with.

The first such infrastructure protection is called *situational awareness*, which involves the procedures and practices for a security team to maintain accurate knowledge at any given time of the intensity of threat to large-scale system support. Such a goal has no meaning in smaller systems. Situation awareness of security for your PC, for example, would be excessive – perhaps even weird.

Achievement of such awareness is best done through all-source data collection, usually into a *security operations center* or *SOC*. The purpose of a SOC is to provide a centralized means by which collected data can be combined, stored, and subjected to analysis. The analysis is intended to uncover subtle clues about possible cyber risks.

A typical SOC is a combination of people, process, and tools, often co-resident in the same physical space – although SOCs are increasingly being virtualized to take advantage of distributed talent around the world. The SOC operates in real-time, with the stated objective of maintaining situation awareness of exactly what is occurring in the context of the infrastructure being protected.

The all-source collection referenced above includes data feeds directly from the infrastructure being protected, as well as from relevant ecosystem components in the environment of that infrastructure. Public and private feeds of threat intelligence are useful for enhancing the correlative processing required to extract insights from data.

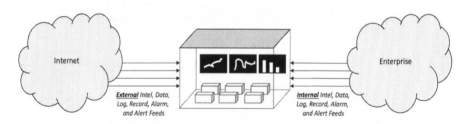

Figure 30-2. All-Source Data Feeds into SOC

An additional security protection for critical infrastructure that has shown promise in large-scale environments involves the use of *deception*. The idea is that by creating fake systems and services, potential attackers are lured into a trap from which they might expose information about their attack methodology – and even in some cases, their actual identity.

Typical deception involves three steps. First, the deception must include a lure into which the intruder steps. Second, the deception must include enticing content, often called a honey pot, that will keep the intruder in place for sufficient time. Third, the deception must include sufficient means for observing intruders to determine attribution, methods, and intent.

A common deceptive method involves a so-called *tarpit* that creates fake network resources to detect and thwart malicious scanners on a network. The way this works is that an entry-point to a fake network is created, and is designed to be expansive, to slow any scanner to a crawl. Virtual technology helps create such fake network infrastructure without requiring new hardware.

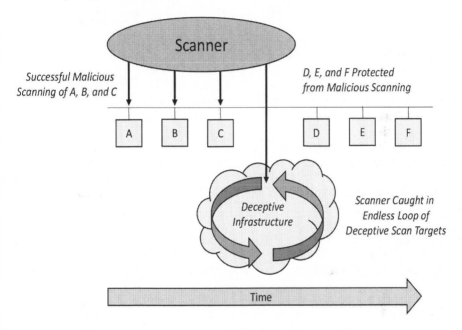

Figure 30-3. Deception-Based Mitigation of Malicious Scanner

Additional techniques exist for protecting critical infrastructure beyond all-source data collection, situational awareness, and deception, but space prevents full coverage here. Suffice it to say that this area will increase in relevance as more critical aspects of our society are exposed to the risk of highly capable adversaries with intent to bring damage to these essential services.

To summarize: Critical infrastructure involves support for services which if removed would cause serious problems for society. These include power, energy, telecommunications, finance, and government. Security for infrastructure, such as situational awareness and deception, tends to be different than one finds more commonly in smaller systems.

Made in the USA
San Bernardino, CA
03 December 2019